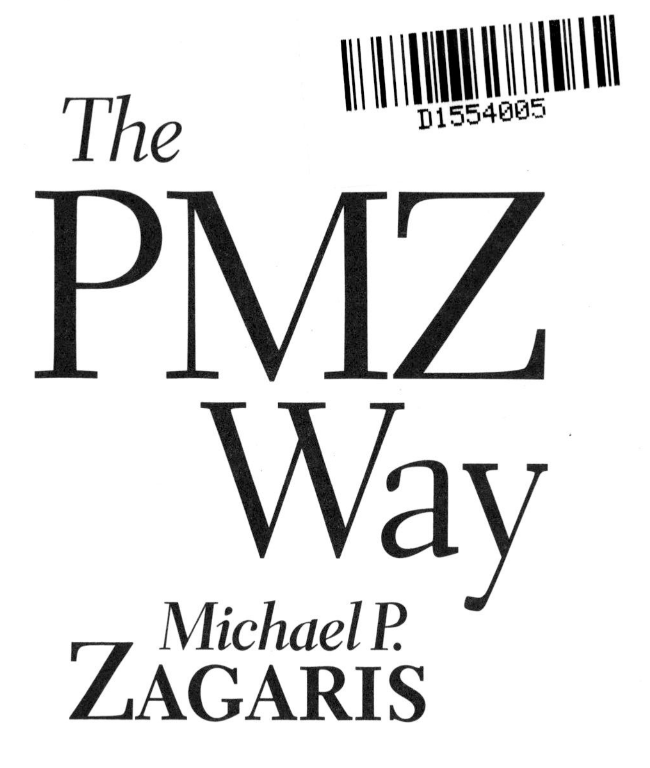

The PMZ Way

Michael P.
ZAGARIS

Strategies of Highly Successful Real Estate Agents

PMZ PUBLISHING

Published by PMZ Publishing
1120 Scenic Drive
Modesto, CA 95350

First printing March 2005
ISBN 0-9766088-0-4

Printed in the United States of America
10 9 8 7 6 5 4 3 2 1

Library of Congress Control Number: 2005901220

Cover design by Roy McKenzie

Photos by Jeff Broome and Kelly B. Huston

The PMZ Way

Strategies of
Highly Successful
Real Estate Agents

Table of Contents

Acknowledgements

I have been blessed in my personal life with an extraordinary family and in my professional life by an inspiring team of real estate professionals. In these pages you will find the stories and insights of some of the dedicated agents with whom I have been fortunate to be associated.

Although I always felt I knew these folks pretty well, during the course of preparing this book I learned so much more about them and what they have to contribute. In that sense, it has been a great learning experience for me.

Time and space do not permit me to include the stories of scores of others who are equally as deserving. I am lucky to have had the opportunity to know and work with them all.

PMZ Real Estate is named after my father, Paul M. Zagaris, the founder of our company. There is no way I can ever adequately express my gratitude to him for all the learning and wisdom he imparted during his lifetime. I am also indebted to the memories of my mother, Liberty, and my brother, Steve, whose love and support I shall always cherish.

I am grateful to my partners in business: my sister, Paula Zagaris Leffler, and my brother, Jon Zagaris, for their support and leadership on a daily basis as we work together to continually transform our family business. Let me also thank my brother-in-law, Duke Leffler, and my sister-in-law, Grace Zagaris, for their significant contributions to our family business.

I am grateful to my partner in love and in life, my wife, Midge, for everything.

Finally, my sincere thanks go to Marc Grossman, a Sacramento writer and media consultant, who helped me shape my words and thoughts as well as the agents' stories into this book.

Preface

The PMZ Way

This book is for you if you are considering real estate as a career or if you are already in the business. My hope is that you will benefit from my words and the real life experiences of the agents whose stories are found in these pages.

My father, Paul M. Zagaris, grew up in the coal mining camps of Wyoming. He was forced to work in the mines after his dad died in a mining accident. In 1947, after serving in the U.S. Army during World War II, he brought his family west to California's Central Valley, obtained a real estate broker's license and began his career. I have fond memories of tagging along with him when he held open houses as far back as 1952, when I was four years old.

This book contains lessons I learned from my father and from the many extraordinary real estate professionals I have been fortunate to work with over the years. These lessons, acquired over nearly six decades of observation and experience, have been woven into the fabric of our culture at PMZ Real

Estate and have become what I call "The PMZ Way."

Men and women come into the profession from a variety of backgrounds. Some have just graduated from college. Others have had prior work experiences in which they were an employee of a business or organization typically unrelated to real estate.

What attracts them?

Many see real estate as an opportunity to better themselves financially and enjoy greater control over their own destinies. More often than not they are lured by the prospects of financial gain during a healthy real estate market. They see the benefits of buying and selling houses all around them every day. If owning real estate is a good idea, they reason, then it must also be a good idea to work in the industry.

At the moment of this writing the real estate market is stronger and more vibrant than at any time in the past. New agents are pouring into the business, but things will change in the market. They always do.

So if you are considering real estate as a career and are worried that the market might be headed for a downturn let me assure you of two things. First, you are right to understand that the market is cyclical and there will be downturns. But from the perspective of real estate as a career path, it doesn't matter. Success for individuals serious about making real estate a career is unrelated to market conditions.

In fact, it turns out the best time to enter real estate as a profession is when the market is experiencing a downturn. Agents who start their careers during a downturn discover a better learning environment. The fish don't jump out of the water into your boat during a downturn. So do not let the market cycle interfere with your sense of when opportunity exists.

Those who survive and prosper in the industry

learn how to do real estate the right way. That is the purpose of this book: to demonstrate The PMZ Way.

Regardless of market conditions real estate is always a great career opportunity. So enjoy my book and enjoy your real estate career.

Chapter One

Act Like a CEO

One of the biggest misconceptions people have entering real estate as an agent is the notion they are going to go to work for a real estate company. Agents need to see themselves as self-employed individuals establishing a strategic partnership with the real estate company they choose to work with.

Those who go to work with a real estate broker thinking of themselves as employees will significantly limit their potential in the business. Unless they realize they are driving their own bus, they cannot achieve the level of success most envision when they seek out a career in our field.

Still, it is natural to assume the posture of an employee. Most people in the working world think of themselves as employees; it is what they know. Such people can take up space at a real estate brokerage firm and work in the industry, but they will never be "stars" or leaders. While a key decision for agents is which brokerage firm to associate with, an even more important decision is how they see themselves at that company.

The challenge is for agents to see themselves as the chief executive officers of their own businesses. Instead of thinking of themselves as going to work for PMZ Real Estate, they need to say, "I'm my own boss and I'm making a strategic decision to partner with PMZ."

The psychological distinctions between employees and the self-employed are momentous.

They make all the difference in being successful over time. If you genuinely embrace the notion that you are a self-employed individual and the CEO of your own business, you are simultaneously accepting responsibility for your own fate and future. Contrast that concept with those who view themselves as employees, who perceive themselves as individuals following the instructions of others, as men and women whose fates and futures are dictated by how well they serve their superiors.

It is all about mindset. If you think you are the boss and the future is in your hands, then you recognize your real estate broker as a strategic partner and not an employer. If that is the case, you are well positioned to take advantage of the ample opportunities this career presents. There is still much hard work ahead, but you have taken the first big step to success.

You're the boss. You may succeed or fail. But you're going to do it yourself.

There are also significant legal and tax differences between being an employee and being a self-employed person. You are required to pay both sides of Social Security; forward all state and federal taxes, usually on a quarterly basis; and separate personal from business income and expenses in order to properly take business deductions.

OK, now you realize you are self-employed and not taking directions from someone else.

This doesn't mean real estate is easy. It is a serious undertaking. Nobody is going to develop a plan of action or a path to success for you. You are responsible for creating and executing your own business plan and setting your own calendar.

It is vital for each real estate agent to craft a set of goals for him- or herself. Every agent should carefully think out and put together a five-year plan incorporating career as well as family and personal goals. Agents should decide the level of business activity they can realistically expect and how that level of activity will rise over a five-year period.

Then this five-year business goal needs to be supported by a series of one-year plans that let you move towards meeting the long-range goal. Finally, each Friday, agents need to write out a plan for the following week that is consistent with realizing their one-year plan.

The level of anticipated business activity can be quantified in different ways. Agents can stake out a level of income, the number of transactions or a volume of sales in any particular year.

New agents should seek the advice of seasoned industry colleagues in figuring out what goals make sense for them. At PMZ, we encourage our people to set goals in the range of 12 completed real estate transactions, or homes sold, in the first year, with that number increasing by 35 percent annually over the first five years.

Using these recommendations, agents would complete 12 transactions the first year, sell 16 homes the second, 22 the third, 30 the fourth and 40 in the fifth year. If a person embraces these goals, in today's real estate market he or she could achieve a projected gross personal income of approximately $70,000 in the first year. By the fifth year, gross income could reach in excess of $300,000.

That sounds pretty ambitious, but it is achievable. Some people can do even better. You can set whatever goals you like. But you should adopt a goal reflecting anticipated income and the volume of sales or the number of transactions for each year in your five-year plan.

Moreover, your plan needs to cover more than numerical objectives. It should also encompass what needs to be done to further your career development, including the additional education all of us need to expand our horizons and sharpen our skills.

The education agents receive in order to obtain their real estate license is important, but it is largely unrelated to the skills they require to be successful real estate practitioners. The learning directed at getting a license primarily concentrates on issues of concern to the state department of real estate. The government wants to be sure agents know how to conform to the myriad state laws governing real estate. Such instruction is less focused on the actual practice of real estate per se: what it takes to mount a successful career, seek out and develop a clientele and work effectively with people.

This leads to a fundamental misconception among some agents who have recently earned their licenses: They think they know how to perform real estate. It's not necessarily true. Receiving their real estate licenses merely means they have the knowledge required to pass the state test.

Therefore, it is important that all real estate professionals embrace a life-long learning process early in their careers. At our firm we make available to all agents a comprehensive in-house training process through PMZ University. It features a weeklong orientation course for new agents as well as ongoing classes every day of the week on a host of practical topics for both new and experienced sales professionals. Additionally, there are numerous outside sources of continuing education for agents from community colleges and universities to specialized authorities within the industry who regularly sponsor seminars.

Other goals for new agents should encompass personal aspirations and commitment to family, health and community. It is crucial if an agent is married to have the full involvement and support of the spouse. This is particularly important given the personal sacrifices of time and effort that are frequently required during the initial years when agents are building up their practices.

Among personal goals may be having children, sending them to college, building a home or taking vacations. All impact the level of achievement necessary to realize them. Crafting a five-year vision of what agents want to accomplish in their personal lives—homeownership, college for kids—is just as important as fashioning five-year goals for their professional development.

PMZ Real Estate has actually crafted a set of forms designed to aid agents in preparing, executing and monitoring their business plans. For example, a one-year outline helps sales professionals set out their planning objectives on an annual basis. It asks agents to establish specific goals ranging from the number of transactions, average sales price and total volume to the number of listings they will close and presentations they will make. Other forms help chart their individual progress during the course of each month and year.

In real estate, effective agents need to consciously

plan their day, month and year in advance; they must know ahead of time what they are going to do.

In summary, if you're going to be your own boss, you need to create your own plan, execute it and monitor the results. This is what accepting responsibility is all about. Going into real estate isn't easy. It requires maturity. No one's going to make you do what it takes to be successful except yourself. You have to be a self-starter.

I have stressed the importance of being your own boss, but this doesn't mean you have to re-invent the wheel, starting from the beginning and learning the essential lessons of the business the hard way, by trial and error. Today's agents can benefit from the experiences of successful practitioners who have come before.

Any number of productive PMZ agents qualifies as successful practitioners. Here are just a few of their stories in their own words.

❖

PHIL SCHMIDT: *'On a mission'*

Phil Schmidt has been in the business longer than I. He learned real estate from my father, PMZ Real Estate founder Paul Zagaris. Phil is one of the highest-performing agents in the country.

I went to high school with Paul Zagaris' sons, Mike and Steve. Our mothers played bridge together. When I graduated from school, there was no question where I would go to work. I was one of the youngest agents he ever hired. When Paul Zagaris died, I felt his loss as much as his own family.

My father at one point was a very large and successful farmer of tomatoes, melons, cabbage and lettuce. He never owned the land; he always leased.

When I was in the eighth grade his packing shed burned down and he went bankrupt. Dad had a sixth grade education, but he was a great farmer. When the shed burned and he could no longer farm, a friend told him he could be a successful ranch broker. That's what he did in a new career starting in the 1960s. I found it fascinating. He made as much money as he had at the peak of his farming career and enjoyed being the CEO of his own business. He had such a good relationship with other farmers that when they needed to sell land, they turned to my dad.

Then he sold homes. I thought to myself, "This is pretty cool." Outfits like the Bank of America were recruiting my friends in business school, offering the chance for big money and nice cars. I thought, "What do I want to do?" I was leaning towards wanting to be in real estate, but I wasn't sure.

I was 23, and had just graduated from college at Fresno State with a degree in real estate and urban land economics. I was going for a master's degree, had been injured in a water polo accident and had to drop out of graduate school. I did have a broker's license already because my education counted as two years of experience.

So I moved home to Modesto in 1974 with no money and a typical college student's Volkswagen. I called Paul Zagaris and said I needed to talk with him. "I have a B.S. degree and broker's license," I said. "I can't go back to school." Paul asked if I could be in his office in five minutes and hung up.

I was there in three minutes. I didn't have any nice clothes to wear. When I walked into the office, he said, "Phil, I'm going to be in a meeting for 45 minutes."

He was testing me. He told me to talk to his sales manager and partner, Dick Jones.

Forty-five minutes later, Paul asked Dick Jones what he thought about me. Then he turned to me and said, "Phil, be in the office at 10 a.m. tomorrow and buy new clothes."

The next day, Paul Zagaris was sitting across the desk from me and asking, "Are you willing to work 26 hours a day, eight days a week the first year of your career?"

Paul hired me as an agent. I had no idea what I was getting myself into. No clue.

If you want to make real estate a career, you have to stay focused and can't deviate from your daily plan and routine. This is probably true with any career. When you're the CEO of your own company, your success is all about your ability. You can't blame anyone else except yourself. As Paul Zagaris said, "Your only competitor is whom you wake up and shave with in the morning: the guy you look at in the mirror."

For me the discipline was easy. I was an athlete. I was used to getting up at 5 a.m. each day to go and work out for water polo—swimming laps from 5 to 7 a.m. and then going to class. When you're a college athlete, you're on a schedule. You need to get in your workouts, your education and do your homework to pass classes and maintain a certain grade level to stay in school athletics.

I never lost focus. I was there on a mission. So when I went into real estate, it might have been a lot easier for me than for others.

Every day I went out, bought the newspaper and called for-sale-by-owner ads. These are people trying to sell their homes by themselves. I'd try to get them to list their homes for sale through PMZ Real Estate and me. I wanted to represent them in the sale of their homes. I wanted to put PMZ's blue and gold sign up on their front lawns and get their ugly signs out of the ground.

It wasn't always easy. At that young age, I found everyone's story pretty consistent. A lot of sellers never had a good experience with an agent for a variety of reasons and so they thought they would try it on their own.

The bottom line was, I found many for-sale-by-owners didn't mind working with an agent. Handling their own listing is a way of shopping for one. They're looking for someone who will click with them.

I did that for several years. My success rate was really high. I was empathetic with their stories. I told them I didn't want anyone to have a bad experience with me; it should be a good experience.

When you're selling someone's home you must handle it with the understanding that what is at stake is the biggest investment of a person's lifetime. It's our job to protect that investment and make sure their best interests are represented. I tell them that from the get-go. If I fail, I say, I deserve to be fired. Actually, I've been fired only once or twice in 30 years, and then by mutual consent. I'd rather have friends than enemies.

I would host open houses every Saturday and Sunday at the homes of my listings. Additionally, if there were homes where I didn't have the listings, I would ask other agents if I could hold the open houses for them. This allowed me to meet people walking through who were looking for homes and didn't yet have an agent.

If they hadn't met or weren't working with an agent, my goal would be to develop rapport and a relationship. Then I'd ask them, "If you're not working with an agent, would you be interested in working with me?" I'd schedule an appointment, do the pre-qualification, get in the car and find them a home.

All these are basic fundamentals of real estate sales that always work regardless of whether it's a good or bad market.

You can't sit at your desk and expect the phone to ring. You have to go out and make business happen —in a normal market. Of course, in today's market agents can sit during opportunity time in the office, answer the phone, be unconscious and make a living. Today, people are calling because demand for real estate has never been higher. But in a normal market you have to work to make the phone ring.

I also became heavily involved in the community. I served on boards of directors, joined the Kiwanis Club and was an active member of the Chamber of Commerce. I was really involved with my kids' athletics and in their school. I've been doing it for 30 years.

People knew I was the type of guy who, once engaged in things, became truly committed. They assumed my seriousness in participating with community groups carried over into my seriousness towards my career. It produced a lot of referrals. People I met who wanted to buy or sell a home would call me or have their friends call me.

My career has been built around my sphere of influence. Both have grown enormously, from first-time to last-time homebuyers.

I also benefited enormously from Paul Zagaris, a true visionary who taught me to listen to the people who have been there. Too many people in real estate who do not have a mentor or a plan expect things to just fall into their laps without any effort on their own behalf. That's a fantasy. It's not going to happen.

Now, there are people making more money than they ever thought they would in their entire lives because the current real estate market is great.

When the market changes, as it always does, those people will wonder what happened because they only experienced an exceptional market.

That's where skill and hard work come into play. If you're not used to doing the basics because you haven't had to do the basics, then you will soon be out of business. Look, today there are 370 homes for sale in Modesto. And there are more than 1,000 agents. Somebody is not eating.

What I learned from working at PMZ Real Estate under Paul was you couldn't deviate when you're beginning in the business. To be successful you have to make a lot of sacrifices, all the time. It's like being an M.D.; you're always on call. When you're just starting out and a client calls and says, "I want to list my house Saturday at 3 p.m.," you have to be flexible enough to re-adjust your schedule.

Paul made me put up city maps with my card at every gas station and restaurant near the pay phones. One Saturday my future wife and I were about to take off on a trip to Yosemite. We were getting in the car when the phone rang. I looked at Teresa and she was saying, "We've got to go."

It was a couple at the Denny's restaurant on McHenry Avenue in Modesto. "We're in town for just a few hours," the caller said. "We've seen a few houses. If you could make a few appointments to get in to see some homes, it'd be terrific."

When I walked outside, Teresa could see by the expression on my face that our trip would be delayed by a few hours—not cancelled, but delayed. When I saw the couple a short time later I said, "You caught me just in time," and explained I was on the way out the door to go out of town. I took them around and they found a house they really liked. I submitted the offer to the other agent. It was a good offer and I told my clients they had a deal and I would talk to them on Monday.

Those are the types of sacrifices you have to make regularly, especially at the beginning. That's one way to show your commitment. Those people never forgot that I postponed a trip to help their family buy a home in Modesto. They bought that house for around $20,000. I've sold them three houses since then. I can't tell you how many referrals they've sent my way.

You have to work with a good attitude. A lot of agents who received that call on a Saturday morning would have reacted with frustration. You can't get mad. My gosh, the broker invests a lot of money so his agents can be successful. The Zagaris family is always spending a great deal on marketing tools for their agents. We have a state-of-the-art web site, state-of-the-art offices with the latest in technological advancements. PMZ University is amazing in itself. No one can compete with us when it comes to promotion and advertising. We are surpassing expectations far beyond belief.

People want to come to work with us because of the great things our brokerage company does for its agents that other brokers don't do.

It all gets back to what Paul Zagaris said to me years ago: "The only thing that sells real estate is shoe leather." You have to go out and walk the walk and talk the talk. You have to meet people. Paul was incredible, the mentor of all mentors for me. He took me under his arm at age 23 and was hard on me for a reason. He wanted me to succeed as much as I did. He saw my potential and talent more than I did.

I was devastated when he died in 1980 at the age of 60. My only regret is that I never had a chance to thank him.

If you listen to the things he had to say, you would succeed. And if you don't, you weren't meant to be in this business.

❖

Richard Domagalski: *Sticking with the basics*

Richard Domagalski has successfully been in real estate for more than 10 years, five of them with PMZ Real Estate. He works as a team with his wife, Mary.

Most people leave their jobs to come to work in real estate because they are tired of people telling them what to do. They think they're going to make lots of money and not have to work very hard for it. They don't have a clue about what it's like to be in business for themselves. They think of it as going into real estate instead of being in business. They don't have a real sense of being self-employed.

Many of them also don't want anyone to tell them how to do it or tell them how many hours they need to be at the office.

Brokers see agents as their customers. The broker's job is to keep us happy. Unfortunately, across the industry historically a lot of brokers would rather keep the majority of their agents happy even if they were not very productive versus keeping the agents happy who are very productive in the office. In an office with 50 agents, 30 of whom are not doing much, most brokers would rather lose their productive agents than upset their unproductive agents.

Mike Zagaris talks about the need to be out there prospecting and working past clients. The business has gone from a transactional market into a relationship market. Up until the last three years, the market was about transactions: banging out deals. Now there are still hundreds of agents doing hundreds of deals and a slew of agents doing very little. The average agent nationwide is selling four houses a year. That's not a living. These agents are getting in the way of agents who actually work for a living and are committed to making a career out of this profession.

Part of the challenge from the broker's point of view is hiring enough people, culling through them and retaining those who are good at what they do. You want agents who know how to run their own business, show up every day and have a real plan and specific goals. They also need to have something inside them that drives them every day to want to be successful.

Mike has recently been warning his agents to be prepared because a big turn in the market is in the offing. It can't keep going with these current prices without some kind of adjustment. Interest rates have been our blessing. They are edging up. In the next few years they will be edging up even more.

You have to track your results. Every single day, agents need to track what they do. When I show up at the office, part of my daily plan is talking to so many people a day and prospect so many hours each day. You can call "expireds," homes that were listed with other brokerage firms that have come off the market and are now open game for another agent to solicit and try to get the business. You can call past clients and find out if they are interested in buying or selling or if they know someone who is.

It's all a numbers game. If I make X number of contacts every day, I know that will generate X number of leads leading to X number of appointments, leading to X number of sales and closings. If you don't track your numbers, you don't know where you're going. You need to be monitoring your business.

Every successful business does this. Many in real estate haven't historically done that because many have never been properly trained to do it.

It's a discipline, a mindset, replacing one habit with a better habit. It is what I call repetitious boredom: doing the same thing every single day, hitting the numbers on the phone or meeting face to face at the door.

There are only three ways to get business in real estate: Buying it by advertising or conducting open houses; waiting for it by having agents at their desks doing "floor time," sitting for hours and waiting for calls to come in; or working for it by going out and finding somebody to do business with.

I opt for the third way. Somebody once told me you should never need a deal, but you should always be looking for one. Boy has that worked for me.

I'm now at the point as a seasoned agent where my business has changed. You can get yourself into a lull because you're not returning to the things you did at the beginning.

I have to remind myself all the time to stay humble. You keep yourself humble by remaining grateful for what you have and what has been given to you. The more I feel grateful, the more it humbles me to know I didn't accomplish this on my own.

No one goes into real estate to be a loser. Everyone wants to make it big. But if all they think about is making it big, it won't happen because their priorities are out of order.

This business should be about the people who trust us with where they want to go with their lives. It's a very big trust. You can't think that this business is only about me and that all I care about is making money. I always need to re-evaluate where I'm coming from. My wife is also very good at keeping me humble.

❖

MATT KEENAN: *Listening carefully and planting seeds*

A former truck driver, Matt Keenan has been in the real estate business for just a few years and has developed a highly successful practice.

I'm a high school graduate from Manteca who drove trucks for 15 years before entering real estate.

Mike Zagaris said I would be able to do it. I thought he wanted me to fill a spot at the desk like the other brokers I interviewed with. But my first experience when I started this venture was a lot of nervousness and fear.

The manager of my old trucking company called and asked how real estate was going. "Terrible," I replied. My old manager said he had a spot open at my former company and I accepted.

So I had all my stuff packed up and was ready to go back to driving trucks. I went by Mike's office and told him, "I appreciate the opportunity to give the real estate profession a shot. It's just not working out. I haven't sold anything in the last few months. I need to provide for my family so I'm going to quit."

He told me to come in and close the door. "What if I met with you once or twice a week?"

"I don't know if that will really help," I said.

"Once a week let's go over building your plan," Mike urged.

After spending a month going over things with Mike and putting into place what he was telling me, I put eight or nine homes in escrow. It wasn't so much what Mike said to me but the fact he went the extra mile to help me make my business a success. I thought to myself, how could I quit on someone who isn't quitting on me?

Mike and I kept meeting. He told me I have to start reading: Business Week, Forbes magazine. He started giving me his old magazines when he was through with them.

Now I'm teaching classes for new agents at PMZ University, which humbles me. Management asks me to teach courses on listing presentations, how to present myself to sellers and how to help them choose me to sell their homes. I repeat a motto I heard long ago: People don't care how much you know until they know how much you care.

I've beaten a lot of more seasoned agents out of properties by simply going and listening carefully to sellers talk. I listen to their concerns, what they're looking for. When someone puts their home on the market, many agents out there don't care about helping them find a place to go. They just care about putting their sign up on the seller's lawn.

One thing that has helped me is that I won't go into a listing presentation by just talking about what their home is worth and how I can sell it. I go into that presentation by finding out where they want to go and what they are looking for in a new home: size, area, amenities and price. Then they see I really care about their needs.

It's the truth. I do.

It can be frustrating and very personal when sellers talk to agents about the homes they fixed up and put all this sweat and energy into.

My clients know I care where they are going and my job is to help them find a place where they can feel comfortable raising a family. It isn't just about sales; it's about helping people get what they want. I try not to be pushy with people; I just try to help.

When you push too hard and try to make quick sales, you don't get that long-term repeat business.

Then you're in this business for the short haul. But if you can get people to realize you honestly and sincerely care about their needs and not just trying to make a dollar, you get that repeat referral business.

During my first two years in business I spent a lot of time—three to four hours a day—prospecting for sale by owners, what they call FSBOs. I'd go online to pull up local newspapers, copy the FSBOs and paste in the numbers for the do-not-call list. Certain people don't want to be called so I don't call them. But I might drop by and knock on their doors. Others who weren't on the do-not-call list I'd definitely call. I still do it. I just got another for-sale-by-owner by calling; it's already in escrow.

I don't think I took a day off during my first year when I was building my business. I worked seven days a week. After that I started taking some days off. But that first year I wanted to be sure I was available to anybody who needed me. It worked well. In the first eight months after I started meeting with Mike I sold 36 homes. The second year I sold 44 homes. This past year I sold 54.

It keeps on getting bigger and bigger with less legwork because now I'm getting referrals. That doesn't mean I don't have to ask for referrals. People will forget about you if you don't ask. I tell people, "By the way, if you know anyone else looking to buy or sell, please don't hesitate to give them my name and number."

Now I get more business with that little phrase than by three or four hours spent prospecting every day. I'll call past clients. Or when I'm prospecting for for-sale-by-owners, if I feel like I've made a connection with someone on the phone, I'll ask.

I get cards or letters from people who say, "You're real nice and if I ever think of buying or selling, I'll give you a call." Sometimes when you prospect, you may not hear from someone in eight or nine months. Then they call and say, "It's time my wife and I want to sell." I just closed one like that.

It's like planting a seed. It can take a long time for the plant to grow. I also call people periodically during the year with information. I'll say, "I don't know if you're aware of this, but a home came up on the market just a few blocks from you. It's comparable and is listed for X." Sometimes that piques people's interest.

Sometimes they'll say, "We're interested but we're just not there yet." I say, "Fine, whenever I can help you get where you want to go, please keep me in mind." When they're ready, they'll call.

You don't get all of them, but your chances sure increase by staying in touch.

Your plans change from year to year. My first plan was to just call and prospect. Different agents are better at different things. My thing is I'm good on the phone. Others like to do it with open houses. I've done that too. But now I value my weekends and taking time with family. Other people are better in person than I am. You have to find your strength and emphasize it.

The way you find that area of strength is by experimenting: phoning, open houses, walking neighborhoods, going door to door, dropping off flyers. At the door it's a real quick conversation: "I just want to let you guys know I just sold a house right around the corner from you."

I personally find it's always easier to sell to someone when I act like I don't care about the sale. I act as if I have all the money in the world. It's like when you're dating a girl and don't want to be too pushy. You want to romance the clients a little bit. That lets the clients know you care more about them than making the sale.

I don't come up to clients and throw a contract in their faces and say "Sign here!" They want to get to know me first. I don't want to go into business with someone who doesn't know me.

So I talk about myself a little bit. I explain who I am, what my philosophy is, how long I've been in business, how long I've been married, the number of kids I have and how I got started in real estate.

Actually, people like to talk about themselves more. So if I can get them to do that, they feel more comfortable with me. The majority of the time it works better when your clients can talk about themselves more than you talk about yourself. If you do that, you will be very successful.

It can be a little hard. Sometimes people don't want to talk. I keep on asking questions like I'm interested, not like I'm performing on stage. And the fact is, you have to really be interested in your people.

My business plan has changed. After a year of not taking time off and prospecting three to four hours each day—with every weekend spent at open houses and walking neighborhoods—I started building up a contact list. Then I would be prospecting people I already knew. For example, at the door I'd ask, "How's your home? How are you enjoying it?" I would not sit down. It would be a quick talk and then I'd leave. It was usually not more than 10 minutes. But after the conversation was finished and the visit was ending, I'd ask for referrals.

You care more about your company a little more when you're not being paid by the hour. You care more about doing a thorough job and completing it. When I was driving trucks for a living, I put everything into it as well. I don't like to do things half way.

That's why my old boss at the trucking company was asking me back. I drove a mountain route. I was picking up and delivering. I would build up rapport with my clients so I could show up late or during lunchtime. When they replaced me they had to use two separate drivers. Even though I would get overtime every day, it was cheaper to pay it to me than to pay two other drivers each for eight-hour shifts.

Still, real estate is way different because I was so used to working on a schedule as a truck driver. Working real estate, I would go to bed at night and couldn't stop thinking about some of the escrows I had going on. I learned to write notes, leave myself messages on my desk so I wouldn't be afraid of forgetting something. It let me sleep better.

I had headaches for months in real estate because I had never used my brain. Driving a truck was all habit to me. I never had much education. I had never thought of myself as an intelligent guy. My dad worked the tar out of me as a kid. I was never afraid of hard work and was always as tenacious as all get out.

This whole experience in real estate sales was a step of faith. I was nervous about the idea of opening my own business, of becoming my own CEO. I was scared. But I had family members who backed me up. Since I was a kid my dad said I should get involved in sales. My wife was behind me. It was important to have family members who solidly believed in me because there were a lot of times I doubted myself. I wanted to quit. My wife and family members probably believed in me more than I believed in myself.

Real estate has been a very prosperous profession for me. I've really been blessed. My prospects are good. And they keep on growing every year. I think it's the result of where the market is heading. I got started at a great time when the market was very good.

I've seen enough agents come and go. I can sometimes pick out the ones who will make it and the ones who won't, although sometimes people surprise me because they don't let their true colors show at first. Mike can tell. He has a real good eye for those he thinks will make it.

He saw it in me. It's a good thing too because I didn't see it in myself.

❖

LORRAINE CARDOZA: *'Service-driven' and 'client-obsessed'*

An experienced agent before moving to Modesto, Lorraine Cardoza has been very successful at PMZ Real Estate.

I had been a licensed agent working in the Midwest until coming here in mid-1996, and joining PMZ in 1997. I see people in this company who are so disciplined and structured. Mike Zagaris is really into prospecting. I had never done business that way before. He said to go out and prospect.

People would say they do it from eight to ten in the morning and from one to four in the afternoon. They would put it in their schedules and do it religiously. I had never done that. I always took every opportunity to build my business, gave it the best I had to offer and hopefully it would lead me down the road to more business.

That's how I built my business two other times. It takes longer, but the benefits come back strong.

I prospect every day of my life. And I always make sure people know what I'm doing. But I don't pick up the phone and make cold calls, with all due respect to other agents who do.

My business is really service-driven. It is client

obsessed. I want to make sure clients have everything they need. In a relatively short time, I have built up a very good business doing exactly that. I expect it to go on and on and on because my base is always getting bigger.

The first year I was here Mike wanted an actual plan. I was beside myself in assembling one. Someone in the office helped me put the numbers together.

I thought they were too low. But it made me conscious about how important it is for me to write out my goals in terms of what I want to accomplish that year: personal, financial and others. I'll set that goal and more often than not make or exceed it.

Up on the board in my office I have posted my goals and below them what I'm doing in terms of units so I can look at them every day. I know I want to save X amount of money a year and do X amount of dollars every year in volume. The volume of gross sales drives me. That's the accumulated total of the sales prices of everything I sold in the year.

When you talk with agents and ask what are their goals this year, you will get one of three answers, in my opinion: sell X amount of units, make X amount of money or achieve X volume of gross sales.

There is no one right answer. I want to do volume. Someone else will use units sold. I don't care what agents write down. When I begin each day I internalize my goal; achieving that goal becomes an unconscious ongoing process. And when you make it happen, you succeed.

There are so many things to do to make things work right when you are taking care of a client. At first I have a checklist. When the checklist is no longer necessary, when it becomes part of what you do and who you are, things become much easier. It becomes part of your personality.

When my husband and I lived in a Chicago high-rise, we'd get in the elevator and before reaching our floor, everyone in that elevator knew what I did. The greatest thing was that I was doing it unconsciously; I didn't have to think about it. I wasn't uncomfortable doing it.

When I speak to classes of new agents at PMZ University, I stress the fact that people can't do business with you unless they know what you do.

Now I have a licensed assistant and she can make extra income by referring clients to me. You either have the ability to do that or you don't. It doesn't mean you can't be an agent if you don't have it. You just have to do it consciously then, almost get a script, memorize it and remember to use it every chance you get.

Someone at the PMZ University class asked how I get things done. I replied using the story of how when we lived in Chicago my husband would always laugh at me because when we got in an elevator or entered a restaurant, I would say, "Wow, what a day. I sell real estate and some days are rough (or easy)." It gives you the opportunity to tell people what you're doing.

The point is that you have to be the driver to create business opportunities. Once you have those opportunities, you need to do something with them; they have to take root.

It takes two; you have to show the client you will take care of them better than anyone else. You do that by actually taking care of them better than anyone else.

For most people, even if they've bought or sold a house before, it's still a big deal. It is their biggest investment. I don't care if the person is a first-time buyer or someone handling major properties. He or she deserves the respect of being treated like it is a big deal.

That means answering questions, getting back to them with requested information, providing a prompt response on offers. They need to be confident you've got their best interests at heart and you're implementing a plan to help them achieve their goal.

I believe my success has been all about service.

You also need to have the old fire in the belly. I was on tour with a gentleman who had been selling for this company for a while. I asked what he thought it takes to be really successful in this marketplace. He answered that you need to have lived here all your life. I replied that I hoped he was wrong or I didn't have a shot in hell.

I don't think that's what it takes. There are people in our industry who have lived here forever who don't do a hill of beans worth of business. And there are those who do phenomenally well and haven't lived here forever.

There is a young woman, Kristi Engel, at our company who joined last year. She is bright and well educated; she had been very corporate in her lifetime. She did $9 million in gross sales during her first year. She didn't know anyone here. It never dawned on her that she couldn't do it.

Those people who can't possibly see themselves not succeeding don't fail. I can't imagine not succeeding, even though I can't give you the A, B, C and D of what it takes to succeed. It's a mindset. It is the old adrenalin rush to just get up and go.

Chapter Two

Thinking Big

Thinking big.

Too many in real estate don't do it. They earn perhaps $20,000 a year. They must pay both the employer and employee sides of Social Security. They might as well be unemployed. They make far less than they would receive at a regular job.

The top 20 percent of real estate agents collect more than 80 percent of the income produced by all the agents in the business.

One of the characteristics that distinguish those who are successful from those who are not is that the highly successful agents all think big.

My understanding of the power of thinking big came through exposure to my father and to one of the great inventors and entrepreneurs of our time, Alejandro Zaffaroni.

Although my dad grew up poor and obtained much of his education a mile underground as a coal miner, he always thought big—both for himself and his children. He would consistently encourage each of his four children to think big and to think positively.

He taught me the concept of leverage. This included both financial leverage—how to control large amounts of assets with modest amounts of money—and more importantly leveraging my personal power. How, although I am only one person, I can achieve extraordinary results if I think big and appropriately organize myself.

After graduating with a Bachelor of Arts degree in economics from the University of California, Santa Cruz in 1970, I went to work at an entry-level position with a company in Sunnyvale called Xidex Corp. A spin-off of Memorex Corp., Xidex manufactured specialty microfilm products for sale to government and large businesses. After a few years and a number of promotions I established a sound career path at the firm. It was a good company with good people. But I didn't find the environment very stimulating.

On a visit home to see my parents in Modesto I ran across an issue of Fortune magazine, to which my dad subscribed. It featured an article about a pharmaceutical research and development enterprise called ALZA Corporation and its founder, Alejandro Zaffaroni. Zaffaroni co-invented the oral contraceptive at Syntex Corporation and at ALZA pioneered the development of drug delivery systems such as the skin patches that are in widespread use today.

The magazine article about Zaffaroni and how he was such a big thinker and visionary was impressive to me. Upon returning to the Bay Area I decided to immediately seek out and obtain a position with his Palo Alto-headquartered company, which is now a division of Johnson & Johnson.

My thinking was simple: I wanted to be around people who were big thinkers. His ideas—and his work—completely transformed the manner in which drugs can be delivered to the human body.

I secured a copy of the Palo Alto Times and searched the employment want ads. There was a position open in production planning at Zaffaroni's firm. I applied, was hired and had a marvelous experience there for five years.

Among other things, I got to know Alex Zaffaroni. The exposure wasn't disappointing. Alex really did think big. He wasn't satisfied with thinking on the margins of life. He wanted to think big thoughts—and he did. I came to truly understand what one person can accomplish when he or she thinks big. The excitement, opportunities and success available to those who think big make all the difference in the world.

I also learned other important lessons. Alex taught me about the concept of perceived value: If you believe in what you are doing and the benefits of what you have to offer, then you can create greater perceived value in the minds of those who buy your products or services.

Among other things, ALZA pioneered development of drug delivery systems, innovative ways of delivering a variety of existing pharmaceutical products into the body for improved therapeutic results. Alex was able to convince the marketplace that the value of the innovations associated with ALZA's work was so great that his products oftentimes sold at prices that were 10 times or more above the competition.

In addition, I learned you cannot accomplish things you can't visualize. Embracing a frame of mind that recognizes the unlimited potential of a particular endeavor is to free yourself to accomplish much more in the real world than you would otherwise believe possible without those big thoughts.

I've become convinced that the real estate profession is a 100 percent mental business. It doesn't require physical labor of any consequence. The performance of people in real estate has to do with the conversations they have in their own heads; it is a mental game. If a person's mindset is focused on negativity, pessimism or limited vision then the results will reflect those limitations. Most people don't draw upon but a fraction of their mental capacity.

Thinking big is a conscious choice. It is a liberating activity, which for people in real estate opens up their minds to opportunities that do exist. It makes it possible for them to create and execute meaningful plans that reflect their true potential.

Choosing to occupy this mental state is very important. You can decide how you view the world. You can decide whether to think big or to think small.

Too many real estate agents are conditioned by their parents or their upbringing, through their own experiences or by the people with whom they choose to associate, to see all the obstacles, problems and restrictions in the world. All that does is limit the potential that is out there.

I have seen it time and time again. We get a lot of people attempting to break into the business who have had drilled into them all their lives the notion that life is a struggle and the odds are they're not going to be more successful than their mothers or fathers. This inhibiting view often comes from well-meaning family members. Sometimes people have a spouse or significant other who doesn't want them to take risks. They fear the loss of security that a regular paycheck represents. They just don't realize that the only security any of us has is found within ourselves.

When you go into business for yourself you

have to believe in yourself—and think big. If you don't believe in yourself—or you are not capable of thinking big—then real estate is the wrong business to enter.

People in our field also need to have a good self-image. They need to have that healthy conversation with themselves.

My theory is that we all encounter negative events and influences in our lives, obstacles that must be overcome. To be successful in real estate or in life it is necessary to take proper note of the negative factors and then learn how to let them go. Holding on to too much negative energy seriously limits the ability to adopt and maintain a positive mental attitude.

Some people endure genuine tragedies during their lives and are able to surmount them and become successful anyway. The question isn't whether you encounter adversity. The issue is how you deal with it. There is much merit in the old adage that says some people look at the glass as half empty and some view it as half full. Those who are successful in a real estate career see the glass as half full, despite the fact they are looking at the same reality as those who see the glass as half empty.

So not only do you need to think big, you must also think positively.

A healthy mental landscape is necessary for another reason. Sales is a people business. Real estate agents are involved with people all the time. The clients with whom they work quickly recognize agents' mental states. People selecting agents are looking for positive, upbeat, dynamic individuals who are confident in their ability to get the job done. If you don't exhibit a healthy mental attitude and a good self-image or if you don't believe in yourself, then no one else will believe in you either.

Prospective clients are not drawn to do business with a real estate agent whose thoughts are dominated by his or her own personal difficulties and problems—someone who exudes a pessimistic viewpoint. Most clients see it and choose not to work with that agent.

However, I know pretty quickly when I'm in the presence of agents who believe in themselves and in their ability to sell—people with a big vision of their own future. I am very likely to want to work with those agents—and so will their clients.

You see, having a positive mental outlook is not only good for you personally. Having a healthy relationship with yourself significantly impacts your external relations with other people and enables you to achieve far more as a real estate sales professional.

Listen to the stories of just a handful of the agents with whom I have been proud to be associated.

❖

TIM RHODE: *'Daring to dream big'*

Tim Rhode went from laboring as a grocery clerk to being one of the top-performing real estate agents in our region.

I was born and grew up one of four kids in the small blue-collar community of Portola, population 1,874, about 50 miles north of Truckee in the Sierra Nevada Mountains. My dad was an elementary school math teacher.

One day when I was 12, my dad bought me a new pair of shoes at Grey Reid's department store in Reno. I soon lost one of the shoes playing in the Truckee River. I remember telling my dad about losing the shoe. He cried. "I only have $12 left for the rest of the month," he said. He got his paycheck once each month, paid the bills and had little or nothing left over.

That left an indelible impression on me. My dad was a great teacher and my mom stayed at home to raise the kids. We were an old-fashioned, blue-collar lower middle class family. But we existed; we just got by.

I didn't realize it at the time, but deep down I wanted to do better. I didn't know what that would be; I thought this must be how you live.

I always liked to sell and make money. At age seven I sold greeting cards going door to door to homes and businesses. I did exceptionally well, better than anyone else. I also mowed lawns and shoveled snow—anything to make a buck.

My parents split up when I was 14. My mom went to live in the Bay Area. I moved around a lot among different relatives. At 15, I sold Kinney shoes at the huge Eastmont Mall in Oakland. Even though it was a part time job, I was their best salesman. I always had great sales ability and confidence in myself.

But I was also becoming something of a juvenile delinquent, getting into minor scrapes with the law. There was no supervision from parents or family. I wouldn't have listened even if they tried. I was a total underachiever, barely graduating high school and never attending college.

I got into the grocery business out of high school, working at Save Mart supermarket in Tracy. I was married at 21 and had my first kid at 22. At one point when I was 24 or 25 and working only part time at the supermarket, I was painting street numbers on people's curbs to make money to buy diapers and formula for two young kids.

Then I got into real estate. I remember when I was traveling back and forth from Oakland, where my mother lived, going to Portola, where my dad lived, I'd hitchhike, ride buses and hop trains. I always loved to watch the path of growth in the cities, seeing bulldozers operating, new housing tracts and commercial centers being built and new things coming up out of the ground. All these things I saw blooming fascinated me. Even as a kid, I loved to play Monopoly. And I usually won.

My mom was involved with real estate in Walnut Creek when I was 18. I'd put out fliers for her. She took me to seminars, including one by Tom Hopkins, a sales trainer and motivator. I remember being fired up but not doing anything about it at that point. I was still too much of a delinquent to figure it out.

In 1986, when I was 25, my mom said she would stake me in real estate if I would quit the grocery business. I was making $13.48 an hour with full union health benefits for the whole family. It had security and it wasn't a bad job. I was scared to walk away from it.

But I took her offer, obtained my license while I was still working at the supermarket and then quit my job. During my first weekend in real estate I listed two homes and sold one of them. I made about a $2,000 commission.

I was sitting in the bathtub at two in the morning so excited I couldn't sleep. I found myself dreaming and thinking, where would this career take me?

I called my mom and told her how well I had done that weekend. She had promised to stake me, putting up the money I'd need to live on for six months. After I told her of my success she let out a big sigh and said, "I'm so glad to hear you are going to make it because, honey, I have no money to help you; you're on your own."

I learned a lot of lessons after that. I put eight homes for sale in just one month, during August, my third month in business. Four months later six hadn't sold and the owners were mad at me. I realized, oh, you have to do it right: list them properly, which means price them to sell, and have the owner stage the home right. You have to make sure the deck is stacked in your favor for home selling, which I hadn't done.

In 1987, a very big thing happened to me when I hit upon Mike Ferry, one of the best in the industry when it comes to real estate sales training. I went to one of his seminars in San Jose. Then I signed up for his retreat, where he assembled the best of the best agents in the country at a hotel in Palm Desert in Southern California for a four-day seminar. I was absolutely flabbergasted by the level of minds that I was surrounded by.

When I flew down for the retreat I thought: I'm the top agent in all of Manteca; I'm hot stuff and they're going to see someone special. When I sat down for the start of the retreat, I talked to the persons sitting on my right and left. One guy was selling 150 homes a year; I was selling 37. The guy on the other side of me was making $400,000 or $500,000 a year; I was making around $85,000.

I was smart enough to realize that I should sit down, shut up and learn. Instead of thinking how great I was, I opened my mind to all the possibilities of these wonderful people who were sharing what they had accomplished. On stage were the nation's top agents talking about the things they did to be successful. When the retreat was over, I locked myself in the hotel room for six hours and wrote a plan with the goal of becoming so successful that I would join them on stage next year.

Holed up in that room, I dared to dream big. Returning to Manteca with that plan, I made key changes that amounted to some ballsy moves. For example, the best known escrow person in town worked at a title company where she handled escrows for all the real estate agents. I hired her to work for me full time, matching her existing $50,000 a year salary along with full benefits and four weeks paid vacation a year. Remember, I only made $85,000 the year before.

I tripled my advertising budget. I came up with my own slogan: Call Tim Rhode and Start Packing. I set out to become a household word in my market area, which consisted of Manteca and the surrounding small communities. My goal was if you thought about buying or selling real estate, you couldn't help but think of me.

I also went through a divorce. Although it was amicable, my ex liked me better as a grocery clerk. She ended up marrying a forklift driver. We still remain very close. I think our kids grew up well adjusted.

My business tripled. I rose up the ranks of Century 21, where I worked, meeting and networking with top agents in the country. I also participated in "mastermind" groups through Mike Ferry. They were the best of the best in the real estate industry at that time—superstars.

We would talk on the phone in conference calls once a month, fax each other our business plans, critique each other and hold each other accountable to make sure we were on track based on the plans we had drawn up.

It made the difference between night and day. Most agents where I worked in Manteca were looking around the office and trying to do a little bit better than the next guy. I was comparing myself to the best of the best in the country—agents like Marshall Redder, selling 500 homes a year in Michigan. That first seminar and the mastermind groups gave me a whole new paradigm of what success is and what I had the ability to do.

The goal set out in my plan was to sell 240 homes a year within about four years coming out of the Palm Desert retreat while maintaining balance in my life. I wasn't looking for a meteoric rise. I sought a consistent doubling of my business. I wanted realistic goals I knew I could hit. I always ended up exceeding them.

During the first eight months of my first year I sold 38 homes. The second year I sold 67. I sold 120 the third year and 165 the fourth. Then I averaged 240 a year for the next 12 years—and started to take a little more time off.

I left Century 21 in 1992. At that time I was No. 6 in the nation for Century 21, out of 65,000 agents. Upon leaving, I opened Rhode & Associates Real Estate, with a team of 11 people who had been with the Century 21 office in Manteca. Business went well. We quickly became the number one real estate company in the town of Manteca. The Century 21 office closed within a year.

I also made the best decision of my life in 1992, when I married my lovely wife, Tina.

The years between 1993 and 1997 were tough times for real estate because the market was down during a recession. Prices were low and people didn't want to buy. I had 125 active listings and it was tough to get people to purchase them.

Then in 1998, I met Mike Zagaris, who I heard wanted to come to town. I called him and said I own a real estate company in Manteca and asked if he wanted to take over my company. Within days, PMZ Real Estate took me over. It was one of the best business moves I ever made in my life.

It freed me up to do what I do best. As owner of a company I was more worried about how other sales agents were doing than the bottom line. Selling to PMZ enabled me to concentrate on listing, selling, investing and playing—having fun, achieving some balance in my life, being a good family man and participating in the physical activities I enjoy so much.

I'm an avid outdoorsman; I love things like skiing, mountain biking, hiking and abalone diving.

PMZ took over most of the management functions and overhead, which were big burdens lifted off my shoulders. I had gotten away from my strengths, which were listing and selling homes. Instead, I was spending the major portion of my time running my own company and trying to help other agents who worked for me do well. My number of listings had gone down along with my inventory and market share. Most important, my net profit wasn't healthy.

Under PMZ, I got back to basics. With help from my accountant and friend, I used what I call key performance indicators: If I do this, this and this on a consistent basis, I will achieve the results I want.

For instance, if I work 18 days a month—not that many days—work 30 hours a week, make 1,000 contacts on the phone and go out on 40 listing appointments, then I will take 18 listings, 12 of them will sell and I will close 10 transactions a month. That was all I needed to meet my goals. This process keeps me on track and makes me focus on the simple things I need to do to make my numbers work.

I used to gross a lot more money, but because my expenses went down so much since going with PMZ, I had far more net spendable income.

As the kid who loved Monopoly, I always focused on investing. My line is that it's not what you make, it's what you do with what you make that eventually determines your lifestyle in the later years. I don't think people focus on this nearly enough.

I bought rentals early on. It was difficult to hold onto them when the market was down, but I did. I owned eight rentals through the early '90s and bought 12 more between 1998 and 2001, from single family detached up to eight-unit apartments. I owe this buying spurt directly to Mike Zagaris. When the market took off, they tripled or quadrupled in value. Now I have a credit line against my properties of $1.5 million.

I now have a side business—tapping that credit line—with a team that buys fixer-uppers, fixes them and sells them for profit. It works really well in conjunction with the real estate business as I have another team in place to oversee and repair the fixed up houses. So I have three businesses: the real estate listing and selling business, the rental business and what I call my flipper business—the fixing and selling business. I have staff people who run each business. All are cross-trained so when one goes on vacation, the others can cover for him. My wife, Tina, does the books for all three companies. Like most sales people, I get really high and really low. What I love about her is she's right down the middle; she keeps me on an even keel.

Now I probably work a total of about 10 weeks a year. I take back-country ski classes, avalanche training and orienting classes—learning how to use a compass and topographical map to figure out where you are in the mountains. I almost look at this outdoors endeavor as a new career. I ran two 26.2-mile marathons in the last two years, in Seattle and San Diego. I don't want to stop growing.

We're building a beautiful 4,000 square foot dream home on three acres in the mountains near the town of Portola, where I grew up. It is in a beautiful new golf course community on a hill. On a snowy day I'll literally be able to hike up my own hill with skis on my back and ski down. All my dreams are right in front of me, all the things I love to do.

My dad and brother still live in Portola. Ironically, my brother recently asked me how I plan to eke out a living up there. I immediately replied, "I don't eke."

When I'm riding chair lifts or mountain biking

in the middle of nowhere I have time to do what most people don't get to do: think, take the time to dream and plan, and map out who I am and where I'm going in my life. Then I can't wait to come back from those activities and implement my dreams. That is what makes me a good businessman, team player, father and husband. The exercise I get gives me the energy I need to accomplish my dreams.

It all began with my mom's prodding to get out of working at the supermarket and get into real estate. Later I bought those rental properties during the recession. I figured out I could do something with my life that was bigger than what I had known.

At each stage I expanded my horizons. Whenever I wanted to do something new, I went out, researched it and found out where to go to learn how to do it right. Now I'm attending more investment and outdoor-related and personal growth seminars.

When the chips are down and things seem to be going against you, you discover the measure of a man. Mike Zagaris has backed me up 100 percent. He's done everything he ever told me he would do.

❖

CHRIS SHAW:
'Achieving the potential I always thought I had'

Chris Shaw is one of PMZ Real Estate's highest-performing agents.

I was born in Oakland in 1952 and raised in Hayward, where I went to school. My father was self-employed and owned a successful tire shop. He retired at 46 years old. Then he got into real estate investing, where he was also very successful, buying and selling both residential and commercial property. My grandfather was a real estate broker in Hayward, starting in 1935. Real estate is in my blood.

After high school I went into the Marine Corps for two years before college. The Marine Corps matured me. I learned a lot. Boot camp taught me how far someone can push himself to achieve a goal. Without that I probably wouldn't be as successful as I am today. It's like cross-country distance running; until you push yourself to a certain point, you don't know if you can go there. Once you do that you know nothing can stop you.

After getting out of the Marine Corps, I graduated from California State University, Hayward with a B.S. degree in business with an emphasis in accounting. I graduated in three years, going four quarters a year on the G.I. bill.

After two years managing my uncle's tire store I entered real estate. I had 26 relatives in the tire business, but the idea of being self-employed, of controlling my own destiny, was drilled into me since I was a little boy. I wanted to be compensated based on how hard I worked rather than on a scale everyone else was making for a particular position.

So in 1978, I got into real estate after receiving my license. A year later I became a real estate broker. It requires an additional examination; the state waives the normal two-year time period you have to be in real estate to get a broker's license if you have a college business degree in a real estate-related field.

I opened my own brokerage office in Hayward in 1979. It was a struggle because the recession hit in 1980. I basically had to support the running of the office myself to keep the doors open. I had 13 agents but they weren't very successful. That recession—with 20 percent interest rates—lasted until 1982.

You had to adapt to what was possible during the recession. Getting new financing was not an option then. Essentially, when we represented a buyer we had to search for sellers willing to carry the loan themselves or allow their loan with lower interest rates to be assumed by the buyer. Otherwise, people couldn't qualify or afford mortgages with 20 percent interest rates.

To get around the high rates I became an expert in creative financing—learning how to put transactions together where buyers would assume a first mortgage from the seller's existing loan. Then the seller would carry back a note that my office would sell to another party at a discount so the seller would be able to obtain most of the cash out of the transaction. It was like a second mortgage but without the bank and its high interest rate. Still, it was very difficult to find sellers willing to do this.

During this time it would take writing up and presenting about 30 offers to get just one accepted. My goal then was to write an offer every single day of the month to make sure I had one seller willing to accept. Eventually I'd find somebody.

This is how I really cut my teeth on real estate—when we were facing such difficult times and tremendous obstacles. I had young children to support and had to just go for it.

The brokerage operation kept going until 1982. Then I decided since I was basically supporting the whole office by myself as the broker, I might as well work on my own and not support all the agents. I became an independent real estate agent, handling the brokerage affairs myself.

The obstacles we faced became an advantage because they taught me a couple of things. First, they taught me about creative financing—and financing is the key to real estate. Nobody pays cash for properties. We always need financing. I learned about financing much more than any real estate agent does today in the business.

Second, I was forced to immediately size up a buyer to determine whether he or she was a viable candidate to work with because it required so much effort to get a buyer into a house I could not afford to work with someone who wouldn't be successful. I was looking for the buyer's commitment to see it through—to see if they were willing to work as hard at it as I was. I devised ways to gauge their motivations, their ability to finance and how willing they were to accept properties that maybe weren't their dream homes.

I took those three criteria and placed them on a scale of one to 10. A perfect score would be 30. I worked with at least three buyers at one time who ranked highest on that scale. This took the personalities out of it. Sometimes agents like to take on a challenge and search for some property that is very difficult to obtain. The buyer's criteria is so specific that it might take six months to find this home where three other agents were unable to. Many agents, especially younger ones, try to save the day and find this perfect property for a young couple they come to love.

I made that mistake too when I was young. You work for months and months and can't find the property. Then I changed and it became a numbers game for me. Because times were so tough, I chose to work with people for whom it was most likely that I could locate properties in the quickest amount of time.

The same is true today. Unless someone is referred to me, I leave the difficult challenges to other agents. I try to work with the best-motivated, financially able people who are willing to look at alternatives.

As an independent agent in Hayward after 1982, my plan was to simplify my life and work lean and mean with not a lot of overhead.

For four years beginning in 1985, my dad and I started an additional business in the East Bay purchasing foreclosed properties, fixing them up and selling them. We averaged two properties a month. There were a lot of opportunities because of the recession. It was very profitable.

Shortly thereafter I moved to Modesto. I wanted a different environment for my five children. They were growing up in the Bay Area where I didn't care for some of the influences. We moved to Modesto because it had a Midwestern flavor to it. The first day after the move we walked into a grocery store and a bank, and people said hi to us. That was not the case in the Bay Area. It felt very comfortable.

I went to work as a real estate manager for a homebuilder in town that also had a real estate office, Grant Realty. Eventually I rose to become vice president in charge of sales and marketing for the entire company, both new homes and re-sale homes.

Then I went to work for PMZ Real Estate in 1992. PMZ was the number one company in Modesto. It offered a home for experienced agents—and had the most successful agents in the area. I wanted to associate myself with those types of people.

My income had reached a plateau for the last few years before coming to PMZ. I had sort of achieved a comfort zone and didn't really know why. Maybe I thought this was what my level was going to be.

So I took a chance in going to PMZ because I knew the agents there were more successful than I was at the time. I figured there was no reason for that. They weren't in the business longer than I was. I didn't think they were any more intelligent, hard working or talented than I was.

But there was something lacking where I had been or there was something they were gaining from PMZ.

At PMZ I found myself surrounded by successful people. Mike Zagaris led them. He was the most intelligent, forward-thinking real estate owner I had ever met. He was talking about developing computer skills at a time when computers weren't really utilized in our business. And he stressed setting goals.

All the agents had to meet with Mike on our goals. The first time we met I tried impressing him with goals that had no accompanying business plan on how to reach them. He clearly saw through that and told me I had to have a plan. He agreed to meet and help me formulate a plan to promote my business and develop my skills.

My best skill is that I'm a terrific salesman. I'm good with people. Mike and I determined that if I was going to increase my business I had to increase the number of opportunities to get in front of people because my batting average, as Mike likes to call it, is extremely high. I just needed more chances to increase my sales.

To better promote myself, I increased my advertising budget, especially in newspapers, in an effort to increase phone responses that I could convert into sales.

My income has increased every single year since I've been at PMZ. I hit my goals each year. Mike encouraged me to set goals that pushed the envelope but were still realistic.

In year one, 1993, my goal was to hit an income of $75,000. I achieved it, finishing with $80,000 that year. It continued to go up each year, in most years dramatically. Last year I made $539,000. This year I'm on track to exceed that.

About five years ago I decided to set my goals both in terms of income and the number of completed transactions. My goal was to eventually hit 100 transactions a year. I haven't quite hit 100. Two years ago I hit 98. Last year I did 99. I feel confident my goal will be achieved.

When I was growing up my father made $100,000 a year. I always said if I could make $100,000 a year, I'd be very successful. I went from earning $100,000 a year to $200,000 the next year and it has been steadily increasing since then.

Why the success? I'm at the highest echelon of this company. I associate with very successful agents. I'm a master at controlling my thinking, not letting negative thoughts interfere with my work.

So much of our success in real estate is tied to how we think, whether we are positive or negative. I'm able to control my thinking. When negative thoughts come in, I'm able to put them away in another part of my brain to deal with later and not let them interfere with my work.

No buyer is going to employ an agent unless they become friends with that person. You have to become friendly and make friends with the client. No matter how technically skilled you are or how well you know the market, nobody is going to buy a house from you unless they like you.

Negative people are not likeable, certainly not for someone who is choosing an agent who will help them make the largest purchase of his or her life.

So controlling one's thinking is really key.

The other thing that happened to me when I came to PMZ was that after so many years in the real estate business I had really become tired and complacent. At one point I was looking at getting into another occupation.

At PMZ I just embraced the business. I focused on goals and when I achieved success it allowed me to strive for more success because I liked the feeling. By accomplishing those goals I also found myself achieving the potential I always thought I had inside me but for some reason couldn't reach before.

I learned some new skills too. Mike uses the analogy that real estate agents are like actors or athletes. The profession requires skills and you have to practice your skills. Actors rehearse. Baseball players take time in the batting cage. We have to rehearse our skills too, so when it's show time, when we're on, we can do the best possible job.

On a day when I have an important appointment with a key buyer or seller, I will frequently take long showers and mentally go through my presentation, anticipating the objections I might hear. The difference between successful agents and so-so agents is the successful ones are able to isolate objections and overcome them. That takes learning questioning skills—asking open-ended questions to get people to talk and really reveal their concerns and interests.

There are studies that show the more clients talk, the more they like you. When I was in a sales presentation as a young agent, I liked to talk and talk and talk to show people how smart I was. I'd eventually wear them down.

Now it's a whole different process. Now, when I'm making a presentation, I take inventory at various points to see who's doing most of the talking. If it's me, I'll stop and ask questions, even if it's about a non-real estate topic, just to get my client to talk.

It really works. It's a matter of them embracing me and trusting me. When I feel it's time for them to make the decision, I'll structure an open-ended question that is compatible with the other questions I've been asking: "So, Mr. and Mrs. Smith, what are your thoughts on moving forward here? What are your thoughts on taking the next step in buying this home?" As opposed to "Do you want to buy this home?" where they answer yes or no. When I ask an open-ended question, it forces them to talk and explain and reveal their true feelings.

Then that tells me what I need to do. If they're ready to buy, we proceed. If they have questions or concerns, my job is to insolate their objections. So I'll say, "Tell me what's holding you back?" And they will. If they don't, I wait for the answer. I make them answer. Sometimes I have to repeat the question. But if I've built up the right kind of rapport, they'll answer it.

Finally, from the time I show up for work in the morning until the time I leave the office, I'm focused on my task. Many agents kind of work at half speed. They will spend time socializing because there is no boss immediately over them saying what to do every minute. I don't work that way.

People who punch clocks work from the time they get there until the time they leave. If all agents had that same sort of dedication, it would increase income by at least 20 percent.

I'm extremely disciplined. There is nothing that will stop me from achieving my goals. Part of that is what I learned in the Marine Corps: being disciplined, having a mentality that no matter how difficult the problem, I won't quit.

❖

VICTOR BARRAZA: *Setting Goals for Yourself*

His is a remarkable story of success at the relatively young age of 35.

I was born in 1969 and raised until the age of nine in a small town in the Mexican state of Durango. My parents were small farmers on their own land. From before I was born, my father came to the United States to work as a farm worker under the Bracero Program.

He went back and forth across the border to provide for our family. At age nine, my family—five brothers and two sisters and I—migrated to Modesto.

My dad did farm work, picking crops like tree fruit and strawberries, and working in dairies. During summers the whole family worked in the fields, except for my mother and the small children. I remember working from the time I was nine, picking cucumbers, cherries and strawberries—and slicing open apricots before they were dried and shipped.

When my two years of junior high school ended in Modesto, I was one of two students receiving an award for perfect attendance, not missing a single day of class. Until I received the award, I didn't realize how rare that was. I assumed everyone had perfect attendance.

At Thomas Downey High School in Modesto I ran track and cross-country and got involved with the Azteca Club for Latino students, serving as its president when I was a senior. I graduated in 1987.

I worked throughout high school on a newspaper delivery route to earn extra money. At 15, during the summer, I worked in the local canneries, canning fruits and vegetables, which was better than doing field work. During high school and for two years after graduation I got a job at Rico's Pizza while attending Modesto Junior College. I started out as a busboy, then made pizzas and later became the manager.

At community college, I took the usual pre-requisite courses. I always thought I'd have a career in art, which I enjoyed tremendously.

Instead, I got into real estate in 1989. I was intrigued by watching late night television infomercials promoting the buying of foreclosed properties, fixing them up and selling them at a profit. I was trying to convince my brother to go halves with me to buy the books and tapes for this course, costing about $400. At the last minute we did not buy the program so it didn't go anywhere.

Then an independent Realtor® who was a regular customer at the pizza parlor told me how well I would do in real estate. He told me I should get into it. He spent time helping me to learn the process.

The term ended at Modesto Junior College. So did my job at the pizza parlor. I immediately went to real estate school, putting in 10 or 11 hours a day. I was able to go through the entire course very quickly. I took and passed the state exam, obtained my license and went to work with Ken Martin, an agent in Ceres.

Soon I was working with a larger broker, Grant Realty, which lasted for a year and a half. That was a great experience because it was the first time I was part of an organized real estate office. We had staff meetings. There were several other agents in the office to talk with. It was great belonging to an organization. Later I worked for Re/Max of Modesto.

Soon I was taking additional real estate training courses offered out of the area, in Sacramento, San Francisco and Southern California, including those by Mike Ferry. They drew people from across California and out of state. I was trained in many areas of real estate, including being goal oriented.

It made an incredible difference. One of the key things that keeps me on track throughout the year is creating goals for myself, making sure they're clearly written out and keeping my goals in front of me at all times. You have to make sure they push you but are at the same time realistic and attainable.

During the first six years I was amazed when looking at my numbers. Every year I did between 170 and 175 percent more than the prior year in sales volume. The numbers of transactions I closed set my goals. They kept increasing as the years went by.

I started my first full year at more than 20. After starting to take the training courses and adopting the goal setting, I moved up to 50 or so a year. Then it went from 56 to 70-some. It reached as high as 118 closed transactions.

One year I was tied for first place among all the Re/Max agents in Northern California, which covered from north of Bakersfield to the Oregon border. That year I had 86 transactions. Richard Damagalski, a fellow Realtor® at PMZ, was the agent I tied with.

That got me pumped up. The following year I did 102 transactions, expecting to win first place at the company. That year a bunch of agents started hiring two or three agents to work underneath them and counting everyone's volume as one. So the guy who won that year had 150; I was bummed. Soon afterwards I found out he had two licensed agents plus an assistant working with him. So for the last eight years, I've had a full time assistant.

Re/Max was sold to new owners. I had been contacted by PMZ on a few occasions to see if I was interested. I talked with agents who worked at PMZ to get their feedback before going there.

Mike Zagaris is a very astute investor and business owner. He has a great vision for the future of the company. He connects with people. And for someone in his position, it impresses me that he takes time to discuss things with his agents one on one.

I've also moved into investments. I bought properties, residential, commercial and agricultural. I currently own 12 residential units on eight properties, including duplexes, plus three commercial buildings and two agricultural properties—almond and walnut orchards—that are managed for me.

In 1991, I began a Spanish-language newspaper, El Sol. It is now owned and operated by the Modesto Bee.

Why have I succeeded? I think it has to do with my overall background, my work ethic, the fact I'm willing to work the long hours if that's what it takes and finally my very supportive wife, Marisela.

I really believe my father and mother built a good work ethic in my siblings and me. All my brothers and sisters are still in the area. Two are teachers in public schools. One works at a processing plant. Another works as a clerk at Modesto Junior college. One manages a warehouse-style store in Merced. Another manages a department at a regional restaurant chain.

I remember when I was in junior high going to school semi-sick. I didn't think anything of it. It was a matter of this is what I had to do so I did it.

Then too, the customer service I offer is part of why a lot of past clients keep coming back or refer business to me.

Chapter Three

Take Care of Your Clients

Being successful in real estate is made far easier when you recognize the importance of developing business from a base of people you know and providing those with whom you work with the highest level of service.

Too many agents and too many real estate industry gurus focus on developing business by cold calling, which is typified by unsolicited telephone calls directed to people the agents don't know. This type of business development does not usually generate a high rate of return.

The reason is simple: the people agents are calling don't know them. No rapport has been established. Yet many real estate sales authorities lead agents down this path.

Most real estate offices feature opportunity time. An agent who is on opportunity time spends hours waiting for calls coming into the office from prospective clients who are not assigned to a specific agent. There is no question business can develop this way. But it is not and should never be a primary source of business. It's analogous to sitting in a boat waiting for the fish to jump out of the water and into your lap. Sometimes it happens that way, but you can't build a career on it. This is not a proactive, agent-driven pursuit. Like other passive types of business endeavor, it is not central to creation of a good practice. Those who rely on such strategies typically fail to succeed in our field.

By concentrating on strategies such as cold calling, agents fail to pay adequate attention to the importance of taking care of clients once they are working with them. The top-performing agents tend to be men and women who understand the importance of working with people they know as well as those who are referred to them by the people they know. The robust nature of a successful practice grows directly in relation to the quality of service agents provide their clients.

What agents should constantly be striving for in a client-centered practice is the combination of providing outstanding service to those with whom they are working coupled with a business development strategy centered on seeking referrals from people who have been well served. That is the cornerstone of a great agent's business.

From a business development perspective, it is far more valuable to center on communicating with people you know, people who know people you know or people for whom you have a potentially valuable message to impart. For example, existing residents in a neighborhood where you have listed a home are often very interested in receiving information about that home. Going door to door to speak with them can lead to dialogue and perhaps establishment of a relationship.

It isn't very productive to call people out of the blue with no useful information, relying on a script and pitch that may not be related to their lives. The best way to prospect is to talk with people you know or have done business with in the past or those for whom you have genuinely valuable information.

I experience this phenomenon as a broker every day I'm developing business by recruiting real estate professionals. People in the business I already know frequently refer them. If I do a good job of taking care of the agents who work with PMZ, they talk well of me.

But here's the catch that many in our field miss: If I fail to ask these people who have a good opinion of me for their help—if I don't let them know I'm interested in their assistance in identifying others who may want to work with me—they may appreciate me, but they may not provide the referrals I seek.

So there are two things I need to do: Take care of the agents who work with me so they're happy and productive. And I need to ask these agents and others I meet for their help in getting me further business.

Agents face the same requirements. First, they need to take good care of their clients. When that happens the grateful clients will say, "Thank you very much. I can't thank you enough." The agents should then reply, "I value your thoughts and would appreciate it if you would do something for me: If you hear of anyone interested in buying or selling a home, let me know." Most of them will.

A great place to start for those just coming into the business is their friends, relatives, neighbors—anyone they know. They don't have to directly ask for business. They only have to ask for assistance—if these friends or relatives would be willing to give some support by providing contacts with people who may be interested in buying and selling.

You don't have to ask, "Hey, Fred, will you use me when you need a real estate agent?" Instead, you say, "Fred, I've set some big goals for myself. And I know with your help and the help of friends like you I can attain my goals. I'd appreciate it if you'd do me a favor."

"What is it?" Fred will ask.

"If you know anyone interested in buying or selling real estate, would you please let me know?" you respond.

Invariably, Fred will say, "Sure."

You follow up that conversation with a communication, a hand-written or printed card, thanking Fred for his support.

Agents who want to expand their practice more rapidly can make a list of everyone they know in the community being targeted—friends, relatives or acquaintances. Then they put the list—and additional contacts that are made—into a database and systematically start contacting all of them.

Every one of us has a pair of eyes. Successful agents recruit scores and scores of individuals in the community to be on the lookout for leads they can refer to their friend in the real estate business. Creating this army of friends and relatives who act on the agent's behalf is part of how a great real estate practice is created.

The best agents spend most of their time on the care and feeding of their referral base and sphere of influence—the people they know through community involvement plus past clients, friends and relatives. It is proper and regular communication with this database and sphere of influence that builds the foundation for the growth of their practices.

Additionally, any time leads are generated from

the database, it is important to call or send a note to those who referred you and thank them—let them know how meaningful it is for your success.

The next imperative in a client-centered practice is once you start working with clients, provide them with the best and most responsive professional service. It's only by providing great service that agents win loyal allies for the rest of their careers. It is by taking care of people that agents ensure people will take care of them.

The most successful agents I know have hundreds of clients they have served well. These clients feel good about the job the agent did for them and are confident the agent will do a similar job for anyone they refer. It is important for the agent to stay in regular communication with former clients, asking for their ongoing help through referrals.

The most successful real estate agents weave themselves into the fabric of the communities in which they live and serve. They are actively involved in charitable, community, religious, civic or political affairs. Many agents coach soccer and Little League. Because of this participation they come in daily contact with lots of people. That definitely increases the number of their acquaintances and it can dramatically expand their sphere of influence.

Agents take part in these activities because they are meaningful in and of themselves. You don't coach soccer for your kids or join a church just to get more business. But as a result of giving selflessly of your energy and time, you come to know many like-minded people who come to know and trust you—and ultimately, when the time is right, do business with you or refer business to you.

There is another key element to a client-centered practice that is often overlooked: the nature of the relationship between agents and their clients.

Agents are getting paid to provide a service. Therefore, they have an obligation to be sensitive about how their clients think and communicate.

Ever meet someone with whom you have an instant rapport—someone with whom you instantly feel at ease. It can be a person who coincidentally shares your mannerisms. Or it could be someone who is so perceptive that they adapt their own communication style with your own to strike an immediate bond. Such people have mastered the internal technology of analyzing human communication and applying it in their relations with others.

People think and communicate in different ways. They have different ways of relating to the world. Agents have a duty to modify their way of communicating to accommodate the communication style of their clients. This process is called building rapport.

In relationships between friends or spouses there is an equal obligation on the part of both parties to meet one another at a central or neutral place. When two human beings are involved in friendships or marriages, no one is getting paid.

But agents are getting paid to be real estate professionals. It is a fundamentally different kind of relationship. Agents can't expect their clients to change their way of communicating.

Some people speak in visual terms. They say things like, "I can see what you're talking about." When they speak of a home, they comment on what they see, offering visual clues.

Others talk about how they feel; they respond in sensory terms. Such people may say, "I really felt warm when I walked into that home."

Still others respond in auditory terms: "I hear what you're saying."

The job of a real estate professional is to be sensitive to how people choose to communicate and then communicate with them in a manner closely approximating that form.

If their goal is achieving a client-centered practice by taking care of their clients, agents have to go where their clients are. Agents can't expect their clients to come to them.

Any number of agents who work with me have provided valuable insights on these topics. Here are but a few of their stories.

❖

Joseph Bondi: *Becoming Your Client*

Joseph Bondi is meticulous and thorough in how he takes care of his clients.

I was born in Maryland in 1957, but we moved to Long Beach and I spent most of my childhood in Barstow, in the high desert of Southern California. There was very little to do there.

I wanted to get out of Barstow. So after high school and before the age of 18, I immediately went into the U.S. Navy, where I was trained as a dental technician and stationed, where else, at the Marine Corps facility back in Barstow.

When I got out of the service in 1978, I moved to Modesto in the great Central Valley. Low rents. Easy living. The movie "American Graffiti" depicted Modesto. I loved classic cars and owned a classic '58 Ford pickup truck.

After working at a couple of sales jobs—I sold vacuum cleaners door-to-door—I got a job as a chicken catcher. I was one of about 200 guys in 10 chicken-catching crews going through long houses at chicken ranches picking up the chickens to be loaded and shipped to market. I did that for six years.

I became a truck driver for the same company. They moved me up to assistant foreman for the trucking operation. Then a stark reality hit me: I realized I would never go further than I was at that job. I wanted something more.

As luck or grace would have it, the Realtor® who sold me my home, Pat Gray, came by one afternoon to visit. She had just opened her own real estate office and said I had exactly what it takes to sell real estate.

So I drove a truck at night and studied by day to get my real estate license. I took the test in 1985, got the license and went to work for Pat Gray in Ceres.

It was terrible. Interest rates were still high. The market was bad.

I also had a trucker mentality as opposed to a sales person mentality. I was driving a 1962 Ford Falcon Ranchero in 1985. I'd tell people my other car was in the shop. I didn't have money and was living paycheck to paycheck.

It was a difficult adjustment. I was going from very strong blue-collar work into a white-collar business job. I had the heart for it but didn't know how to dress or how to conduct myself.

After six months at Pat Gray's small operation I realized I would never really achieve my goal. Then I met Dean Russell, a real estate broker for a large firm in Modesto, who would become a father figure for me. I went to work for him in 1986.

He taught me not to be afraid to knock on doors—and not to be afraid to tell the truth, even when it hurts in terms of getting transactions done. Don't lie, he taught me. Put it all on the table. He said when you get a bad reputation in this industry the news travels really fast. I like for people to know when I'm on the other side of transactions to be thankful they're working with someone who will do the job honestly and pay attention.

Dean Russell had this great phrase: "Play real estate tennis." What he meant was when you get paper work—or the ball is in your court—take care of it immediately and get it back to the other agent as fast as you can so it is in their court. It's such an efficient way of doing things.

I see so many agents who hold onto paperwork and don't quickly complete a task because they're either lazy or don't pay attention. It slows down the process.

He also taught me that real estate is a job. You come into work at 8:30 in the morning whether you have something to do or not. You treat it as a job. You put in the hours and it will translate into something.

Because of my work ethic, Dean told me, "Joseph, get here at 8 a.m. because the agent on duty might not show up until 8:30 and you can get the calls that come in between 8 and 8:30." I can't tell you how many transactions I got from being there early. There are some people who like to get things out of the way first thing in the morning.

When I had been with him for 12 years, Dean Russell semi-retired in 1997. I went to interview with Mike Zagaris. I knew PMZ was the strongest real estate company in the Central Valley. I had never met Mike but knew him as a visionary.

I found out PMZ is very service-oriented for the agents as well as the clients. That was neat. The staff at PMZ fell over themselves to get me the things I needed to do my job. They made sure the phone lines were set up, business cards were ordered in a timely manner, announcements were sent out to past clients. And they did it all with a smile. It was always a pleasure for them to serve me.

I had a computer when I joined PMZ. Few Realtors® had one then. I shared my computer knowledge with other agents to encourage them to get computers. Mike was fast stepping into the 21st century. He knew what was happening with the Internet, e-mail and computer technology before the rest of us. He had the first real estate website in the city of Modesto and was willing to put together an IT department to help his agents.

Mike never made any requests of me because I already had a good work ethic when I got to PMZ. He'd have yearly goal meetings with each agent. At our meetings we'd talk about where I wanted to go during the next year. Usually my goals were pretty self-explanatory. He gave me suggestions and his blessing.

Over time, my productivity went beyond my wildest expectations. In my first year in the business in 1985, I maybe closed five or six transactions. During my 12 years with Dean Russell, my maximum closing of transactions was 56 or 58 a year.

I came to PMZ during a down market in the mid-1990s. Once the market picked up, I was with the number one firm with the best staff and technical support, advertising and company services—like in-house lending for clients to obtain their mortgages. That provided a great package that could not be matched by any other firm in the market.

There was only one way for me to go: up. In the time since the market picked up, my highest closing year has been 2003, when I did 80 transactions with sales valued at more than $14 million.

What's behind my success? Well, first, all calls are returned. Period.

I don't make the mistake many agents make. If I get bad news and I think it can be fixed in a 24- to 48-hour period, I will bear the pain of the bad news and try to figure out a solution before I call the client. Let's say I'm representing a seller and find out the buyer has some difficulty during the loan process. But I'm not sure it will sink the deal. I don't call the seller and say the buyer may not get the loan. I wait for a day or two until I find out for sure. Often it gets taken care of. If it's going to get fixed, why have the client endure a sleepless night. Instead, I'm the one who loses sleep.

Another thing is I like to tell clients about my life. For 14 years I've been sending out special Christmas cards to clients with a story about how my year went. It talks about everything from the new car to my dog, whose name is Attitude, plus a little about real estate. When people don't get it by December 15th, a handful of past clients will give me a call.

I get a lot of referrals from past customers and because of my sphere of influence. People I work with on a professional level in real estate who are not Realtors® tend to use me as their own agent: lenders, pest control inspectors and contractors who work for many agents. They have a lot of choices, including Realtors® who produce more than I do. It is an honor for them to choose me.

I've come a long way in learning how to communicate. When you talk with people, you have to become your client. When I have a conversation with an older lady, I speak clearly and softly. I'm gentle. When I have a conversation with a trucker, I become the trucker, using tougher, to-the-point language. When I speak with a white-collar professional, I speak in the manner he or she is accustomed.

I call people with titles by their title. I'm working

with a doctor now. I know his first name but I call him doctor because he's earned the title through his education and sacrifice.

When I'm with first-time homebuyers or sellers, I speak with them not as a Realtor® but as an educator. I want them to know what they're doing as they do it and after they've done it. I don't want anyone to trust me so much that they just take my word for it when I say you have to do something or when I say this is how things are normally done. I explain to my clients why things are done this way so they'll understand why I'm asking them to do it.

I tell my first time buyers and sellers that I want them to be so well educated that they'll be questioning me by the time we arrive at the close of escrow. People really appreciate it. The process can be a mystery and very intimidating.

It's great when I have a second-time buyer or seller who had a bad experience with an agent who didn't perform his or her duties well. I love that. It's challenging to show the client how it can be done right.

I ask all my new clients if they have ever purchased or sold a home before and what their experience was with the last Realtor®. Boy, do they like to talk about the problems. My strongest suit is avoiding the problems they had before. My clients don't even know it's happening, but they love it. And it produces a lot of repeat business and referrals for me.

I figure that if they had bought or sold real estate before, they had known and worked with a local Realtor®. But they're working with me now. I ask myself why they're not working with that other Realtor® when he or she had the opportunity to be a lifelong Realtor® for this client? Why aren't they with that person now? The answer is simple: They weren't satisfied.

❖

Kristi Engel: *Focusing on Your Clients*

New to the profession, Kristi Engel is self-effacing but very smart and productive.

I was born in Great Bend, Kansas in 1964, where I grew up in a farming environment. I used to say I'm as boring a Kansas home girl as you can find.

My father worked in the oil fields. My mom was a stay-at-home mom. After high school I attended a small agricultural college in western Kansas called Fort Hays State University, where I graduated in 1987 with a B.A. degree in accounting.

I went to work for Cargill. The largest privately held company in the world, it ranges from agriculture to financial trading—anything to do with food. For 15 years I worked in various accounting roles both domestically and internationally. I also earned a master's degree in business from Kansas State University.

Eventually, in 2000, my husband, our two children and I came to California and settled in Modesto. I was a stay-at-home mom for a year. But I needed to do what God and my background intended me to do.

That's when I met Mike Zagaris and he got me to try real estate. He said, "Kristi, you can definitely do this." I pointed out that this was a new location for me. I hadn't grown up in the region. I didn't know many people around here. But Mike said, "Don't worry, you can do it; those are small barriers."

I got the book, studied it and took and passed the test to get my license. Then I went to work for PMZ Real Estate.

Real estate is very different on the inside than from the outside. As someone who had moved 10 times in the previous 14 years, I thought I knew a lot about buying and selling homes. I found out I didn't know very much.

I discovered real estate isn't really about the business of buying and selling houses. It's about people: Their emotions, what's important to them, their goals and priorities, and how the house they want to buy fits into all of these things. It's different for different people.

For some buying a house is all about getting their dream home or living in a certain location. For others it's just a place to live in.

The emotion behind the negotiating part of the business is also different for every client. I've learned how to change my style and approach, even the way I dress, depending on whom I'm dealing with.

It all goes back to my experience with Cargill. During the same week I could be dealing with the presidents of corporations or the leaders of countries on multi-million dollar ventures. The next day I could be with cotton sweepers in Memphis, Tenn. These are the people responsible for sweeping cotton off the gin floors in the production plants where cotton is baled—the process by which it is cleaned and separated.

I would wear Dockers or blue jeans to the cotton plant because if I drove up in a corporate business suit, the workers wouldn't trust me or deal with me. They wouldn't relate to me—when the truth is I grew up in a very poor family on a farm and I could relate to them more than they would ever know.

As a real estate agent, if I'm dealing with a corporate person transferring to work at the Gallo winery, I don't use the same words, language and presentation as when I'm meeting with a couple who just called because their child was involved in a serious accident and their home is in foreclosure. Your presentation style, appearance and approach should not be the same, in my opinion.

When I'm dealing with people, I know intuitively and can use different examples and ways of communicating—especially vocabulary.

In our industry we get caught up using words such as "escrow" and "title." They might as well be foreign words to people who have never bought or sold a house before. So you change your language to explain the process. You don't say escrow; you say there's going to be another person who will help you make sure the title gets transferred properly to the new owner and all the legal parts of the process are taken care of while transferring the title. You explain it in simple terms.

This isn't about belittling people or making anyone feel bad. You're not talking down to someone who doesn't have an education. We are all very different people with different communication styles and understandings.

When you talk with people who are more analytical, they need to be pursued with the facts; you have to take them more data-based information. They're going to want to see more numbers on paper—what the average sales prices have been, more comparable information—than a person with another type of personality.

When talking to this person, I try to anticipate what else they may ask. Even if they don't know they are planning to ask it or need it, I try to come armed with the information. It gets back to my Cargill days. You may have only 15 minutes with a busy executive. So you had better anticipate what he or she might request and have it ready.

On the other hand, the person with a more

emotional personality may want things with a prettier, more cosmetic feel.

There are parts of Modesto I don't know very well. If there are clients who are interested in buying a house in one of these neighborhoods, I pull comparable sales so I can advise them appropriately on good offering prices. Someone else in my shoes may not need to do that because he or she may be a lot more experienced with the area and know the market already.

I don't want my clients to know I've only been doing real estate for two years. It's about anticipation: wanting to look intelligent, like you know what you're doing even when you don't. It's OK not to know. Then you just have to seek out the information you need.

I do that with listings too. When I'm not familiar with an area, I'll drive out and take extra time to look around the neighborhood where the house is located, especially when it involves specialized customized homes where I haven't done business. Also, I'll talk with my PMZ sales manager if there is something I'm uncomfortable with. I'm not scared to say when I don't know something. I will seek out someone I trust in my office, whether it's the sales manager or another agent, and say, "I want to get your opinion on the market value of this home." And they'll help me out.

You hear people talk about a person's frame of reference. It is everything in your background that creates who you are today. When someone explains something to you, your frame of reference encompasses who you are and what your life experiences have been. Therefore, you need to be provided examples that you can relate to that will make the explanation more meaningful.

You get a sense of how people want to be communicated with. Some prefer the telephone. Some like email. Others need to have it done for them in person. Some need a lot of communication back and forth. Some need very little; as long as they know things are being handled, they don't need to hear from you.

I've found this works both when you're trying to pursue new business and when you're dealing with current clients.

My focus is not on my commissions. I don't even track my commissions. My personal business goals are based on my sales volume and I know what that is.

I can honestly say I completely focus on what's right for my clients to the point that when someone is writing up an offer on a property I'm handling on behalf of a buyer I've said to my client, "No, that's not what you want. We'll find the right house." I don't pressure people to make deals when I don't think they make sense for the client. Right now it's a seller's market and if you don't jump on homes, they're gone. Time and time again I've had clients thank me for not letting them try and buy a property they wouldn't have liked.

I'm also good at helping my clients look for properties. I listen carefully to what they like and seem to pick up on what it is very quickly. So I find buyers properties very fast. I don't waste their time because I'm listening to what they like and sensing what's important to them. Then I watch the market for those homes I think make sense. I work very hard for my clients. They'll tell you that.

Now I am starting to get client referrals. Mike [Zagaris] has received very complimentary letters from clients of mine.

I'm envious of agents who talk about their past

clients. Those are the referrals you want. Then the business becomes more fun because you're working with people you want to work with and who want to work with you.

It takes a long while to get there, but when it happens it's very rewarding. You appreciate it when you start seeing it happen.

❖

PAM HARMON: *Treating Clients Like Family*

I have come to respect Pam Harmon, a native of Modesto with a real knack for the real estate business, as a genuine professional.

I was born in Modesto in 1952, the youngest of three children. My father was a farmer. My grandfather was a farmer. I come from a great, Christian-centered family. I grew up loving the land.

My parents taught me very young the importance of integrity and standing behind what you say. My father taught me how to shake hands using a firm grip. "When you shake hands," he said, "that is giving your word. Never go back on it." He taught me that in past generations when people were selling something to someone for X number of dollars and they shook hands on it, it was like a written contract.

I always kept in my head that what I said and my actions affect what happens next. It could be for something happening right now or it could be for something occurring years from now.

I started selling at a young age. When I was 10, my father had me put together a report to present to the banker on how I would borrow money to buy some cattle. He took me to Crocker Bank downtown. "I'm going to stay in the lobby," he said. "You're prepared. You've done your homework. You show the banker how you're going to pay him back for the money you're going to borrow." I went into the meeting by myself. They loaned me the couple of thousand dollars to buy the cattle.

In the morning I had to go out and bottle-feed some of the calves. Some died on me. At a young age I realized I had a debt to pay; if they kept dying on me, what would I do next?

I was able to raise and sell the cattle and pay off the bank. That was my first venture in financing, in borrowing money and knowing about my asset and debt load.

The next year a farmer was raising watermelons across from our place, 20 miles outside Modesto. They were picking and loading melons on trailers. I went over, introduced myself and asked to set up a fruit stand to sell his watermelons there on Shiloh Road due west of town.

The farmer said I would never be able to sell way out there. "Would you please give me a shot?" I asked. He agreed to give me one trailer load. "You do the best you can," he said.

He ended up bringing me a trailer load of watermelons every day. I don't know where all those people came from. On weekends, people came from as far away as the Bay Area. I made him more money off my little fruit stand than he made from some of the grocery stores.

So I grew up loving both the land and working with people. After graduating from high school and taking classes at different colleges, I thought my major would be accounting because I loved numbers. But I always knew I loved to sell too.

During this time I married and put my career on the back burner while being a wife and mother. We now have two children, a son and daughter, and four grandchildren.

When the kids were junior high school age, I took the state exam for my real estate license, passed it and started working.

I just love my profession. I get the greatest joy out of helping people. My business is truly based on my clients. It goes back to handshaking. If you take care of them, they will be loyal to you. They will tell their family and friends about you.

I've had clients where it took me two years to help them clean up their credit and get them on a budget so they could qualify to buy a home. Sometimes I've talked people out of buying when that's what they wanted to do but I knew they couldn't afford it. Their family life was not together; they had so many financial problems that if the debt load from buying the house was added it would only cause their credit to go down or place more stress on their marriage. I'd keep telling them that even though they shouldn't buy a home right away, they needed to have that as their goal. I encouraged them to save and strive for it. "We're going to make it as a team," I would say.

I prefer the team approach. I work for my clients. They hire me. Sometimes that means helping them improve their financial situation so they can buy a house.

A single mother with two teenagers approached me, interested in buying a home, but she couldn't qualify. First, we met with a lender who analyzed what our situation was. (I always say *our* situation because I become so much a part of their lives. It's really personal for me.) The loan officer said my client needed to clean up some issues on her credit, pay off some debt and establish a record of paying bills in a timely fashion.

That's what she had to do for a while to establish her credit. So that's what we did. I put her on a budget. I held her accountable. I checked in on her every month to make sure the bills were being paid on time and she was saving X amount of money out of every paycheck.

We worked on it for two years. Meantime, we kept looking for houses so I could show her what was out there—to help her keep up on the market and to encourage her. She had to see the light at the end of the tunnel.

We found the cutest little house in northeast Modesto. It needed some paint and cleanup. But it had a solid structure. She qualified after two years. The joke we would tell was that I looked so long that if she didn't buy something soon she would have to get me a new set of tires.

When you wait and want something so bad and struggle and save for so long, you know what it means when you finally receive it? There is great satisfaction. My client is still in that house and doing very well.

I'm so fortunate to be on the sidelines and see that kind of joy and satisfaction. Some of my clients have become like family. They come to Christmas dinner.

People like Craig and Michelle. They were from back east. He came out here to take a job as CEO at a local company. They were flying in and he asked if I could pick him and his family up and show them the town.

When clients come from out of the area, I try to educate them on the city and the area around it. Then over time, whether it is one, two or three trips, I get to know them and have a good handle on their lifestyle and what they're looking for in a home.

I remember this couple to this day. He was reserved. They had adopted a little boy from Korea, Tyler, who was about one and a half or two years old.

We looked for houses for a long time. Michelle, the wife, kept saying she needed to be close to the hospital. I found out she was a kidney transplant recipient, had continuing health problems and needed to always be within a certain number of miles of the hospital.

Craig, her husband, traveled on business all over the world. He would sometimes be gone overseas three weeks out of the month. They had no family here. I told Michelle, "Here's my cell and home phone numbers. If you ever need me, call no matter the time."

I'll never forget one Thursday morning when I was headed into the office for a meeting. The cell phone rang. It was Michelle. "Pam, I need to go to the hospital. Can you take me?"

My husband and I took her to the hospital so many times they thought my husband was her dad. They'd come out into the waiting room at 2 in the morning and say, "You can come in now and sit with your daughter."

She has a new kidney now and is doing well. Since then I've sold Craig, Michelle and their family several houses. They adopted a little girl from Korea. We were at the airport to help them pick her up.

Every other year we have a big barbeque in honor of Michelle's kidney. The last time there were 150 people over for dinner.

That's how I work. It's not for everybody in real estate. I look at this profession as my business. Even though I work with a company, PMZ, I'm independent. The business has to be based on who I am and how I want to take care of others.

That doesn't mean I can please everybody. I can't. I fail sometimes. But as long as I have a love of the profession, this is the only way I can do business.

Do you ever go visit someone in the hospital

and meet a nurse who takes such good care of the patients? Then other times there can be a nurse who is tired or indifferent and doesn't treat people very well. I don't want to be like the indifferent nurse. When I lose the love of what I'm doing, it will be time for me to get out.

I started working in real estate in 1986, originally for a small mom and pop real estate company in Modesto when the market was flat during a recession. It was a good time to come into the business because that's when you learn. When things aren't very busy you have more time to learn how to do it right—to ask questions of other agents with experience who you respect. That's when you want to set your foundation in the profession.

The tough times will come again. Those agents who think it will always be great and easy will have to be prepared.

I was selling about 10 homes a year at first. I learned a lot, but the small mom and pop office was difficult in some respects because it was very controlling and you couldn't expand. In the mid-1990s, I was asked to join Re/Max, which was a giant step for me. I was there for nine months and sold substantially more. Back then, my commissions were around $65,000 a year. My goal for the following year was to make $100,000. Even though the market was still depressed, I met that goal the next year.

In January 2004 I came to PMZ. I didn't know Mike personally except to say hello, although I always knew about the company. They had a lot to offer in areas where I needed help for my clients.

Mike takes care of providing any tools we need to benefit our clients or ourselves. He is very bright, always striving and very goal oriented. I love to hear him talk. He is always educating and challenging us.

This is an area where I feel as agents we really let ourselves down. It is so important to continue our education for our clients and ourselves.

At PMZ, I know I can improve and do more volume. Our market prices have gone up substantially, which means more in commissions. But I try not to place great emphasis on the number of transactions I do. It's charted, but if I only look at that, I would lose what I love about working.

I focus on customer service; client satisfaction is a better term. I don't look at the profession over just the next one to five years. I look at it as something I will do forever. My kids know I will probably never retire. When I'm gone, they will just put a "sold" sign over my casket.

I would like to take some more time off and do a few extra things. I can do that if I permit myself. I have that choice.

Now each year I do a little bit better. I want a gradual increase. A lot of times real estate has its peaks and valleys. But if you have a practice based on client satisfaction, you're more apt to have a slow, steady climb. It's like exercising on a treadmill: you increase the incline and speed over time and gradually get in better shape.

There is one area where I have come up short: Because all these years I did not have a database, I did not faithfully stay in contact with all of my clients. I kept in touch with many of them. But when it comes to hundreds of people, you lose track of some.

What's really interesting is now I am creating my own database with the computer support Mike gives me. I went back a number of years and entered old clients into it. Then I sent out a letter apologizing, saying it has been so long since I talked with them. The letter said I'm still around and I brought them up to date on my life. Emails came back from some of them saying they hadn't forgotten me.

I still get involved with my clients. It could be many months while I'm finding them a home or putting together financing. During that time I go to their weddings or their baby showers. I just got a call from the mom of a client; her daughter's baby was born yesterday. The other day my husband and I received an invitation from a past client to the ceremony for his son who is becoming an Eagle Scout.

That's the kind of joy I get from my work. What other profession gives you the opportunity to interact in the lives of such wonderful people?

The only negative aspect of the profession for me is you can't be close to all of them. You only have so much you can give. You get with them and talk to them regularly over many weeks. Then, once the transaction is finished, it's like a withdrawal. It's like when your child goes away to college and all of a sudden you have to cut the strings. That happens between client and real estate agent. You spend a lot of time together and become attached to each other.

❖

Lane Menezes: *Finding the Right way to Communicate*

He is known throughout the region as "The Ranch Realtor®."

I was born in Patterson in 1959 and lived in Gustine, southwest of Modesto. My parents were dairy farmers and I was raised on dairy and farming. We moved to Modesto in 1967, while we continued dairy farming in the Westport area west of town.

In 1975, after my brother graduated high school, my dad said to my brother and me, "Boys, if you want to stay in the dairy business, I'll get more cows and build a bigger barn. If not, you go for outside work and I'm going to sell the cows." We said sell those cows.

After Ceres High School I went into the electrical business, working for eight years as an electrician doing remodeling work on dairy barns. Then I went to work for farmers, using my own equipment, a John Deere 12-row corn and bean planter. It created 12 rows covering 32 feet at a time.

I was planting beans for one of my clients in spring 1989. He jumped into my tractor and said, "You ever thought of selling?" I sold the planter to him.

I had wanted a career in real estate because of a relative who worked in a little real estate business who was just starting off. He asked my wife and I to come to a new agent orientation. He wanted to fill the office up with bodies. I went, sat down and listened. After the guy got through talking, I told my wife, "Annette, I can do this business and sell ranches for a living."

That fall I was running harvesting equipment for a friend. I ordered a mail order Principles of Real Estate course and listened to the tapes over and over again 18 hours a day while I was in the harvesting machine. When I took the test, I finished in an hour. I easily passed and got my license in February 1990.

I started at my cousin's little office in Modesto. I won all the top awards. I was selling big ranches. My business grew. No one could compete with me.

In 1993, I heard from Mike Zagaris. He sent out a packet of information concerning a small ranch in Escalon to about 20 agents to see if they could sell it. I sent him back a thank-you note for thinking of me.

"I want you to know I sent out packets to about 20 agents and you were the only one who sent me a thank you note," Mike told me. "I appreciate that.

If you ever want to make a change, I'd be more than happy to sit and talk with you."

I thought it was time to make a change. I met with Mike and Phil Levin, sales manager for the Orangeburg Avenue office of PMZ. We sat down and I had 20 questions to ask Mike. Half way through, he interrupted, "You know," Mike said, "I've never been interviewed by an agent. I always interview them."

"This is a big decision for me," I replied. "I want to make sure it is the right move."

"I understand and appreciate that," Mike said.

I made the move. Mike has an amazing mind, a way of translating his ideas and thoughts to anyone he talks with in a form that is adaptable to them. He saw my business and how I ran it. He gave me great ideas on how to put business together. Rather than invest a lot of money in advertising, I go out and talk directly to key people who help other people make decisions. Instead of a shotgun approach, I use a high-powered rifle to meet other people who buy and sell ranches. He supported me the whole way.

I was at the point where a lot of time was being spent on the road. I was averaging 150 miles a day. Now I find myself on the phone, putting deals together with repeat clients who keep coming back.

With Mike's help—through several meetings held over the year—I keep focused on the importance of talking to key people. He has helped me set the groundwork for a good strong foundation in the business that I didn't have before because I didn't have anyone with Mike's knowledge to bounce ideas off of. Other real estate gurus have great knowledge of the business when it comes to residential. But that doesn't apply to me because I sell ranches, not commercial or residential properties. My business is unique.

My volume has gone from $4 million in sales in

1993 to around $12 million a year now. My business has worked up to the point where it is consistent. Mike taught me how to keep it smooth and continuous.

I'm actually a very shy guy who doesn't like to go out and force myself on anyone. I prefer to have people call me and invite me in. It doesn't always work. But you have to communicate with people at a certain level. Mike gave me pointers on how to do that. He also suggested I take the Tony Robbins course.

It's a matter of getting on the phone and finding out what a person's needs are, listening to them and being able to help them without being pushy.

Some dairymen and farmers are very loud. When you call them on the phone while they're on their tractors, there's a lot of background noise.

They'll answer the phone and I'll say, loudly, "Tim."

"Yeah," the guy will answer.

"Tim, it's Lane."

Once that's all done, you can have the conversation with them. You can get so good at matching their sounds and tonality that you could be evil and lead people astray if you wanted to. You have to be honest with people.

A little old lady will say, softly, "Hello."

I'll say, also softly, "Hello, is this Mrs. Robinson?"

"Yes."

"Hello, Mrs. Robinson, this is Lane Menezes."

When it is an elderly person I'll often continue the discussions with a family member (who they feel more comfortable with) handling the matter. It works very well. You establish rapport.

The main thing is to get past the facade within the first three minutes. The person you're calling is wondering: Is this a sales pitch call? Is it a waste of my time? If you can get past that, you can do business with people because there is a trust that builds up. That's where people who are unscrupulous can take advantage.

Some years ago a dairy farmer called wanting me to sell his property. He signed a listing agreement with PMZ. As soon as it was signed, I immediately went out and within hours found someone interested in buying the working dairy facility. Then the dairyman had a change of heart—seller's remorse; he didn't want to sell after all.

I couldn't let the man out of the listing agreement because I'm only an agent; it was up to PMZ. So I spoke with Mike Zagaris. He said that I could legally hold the seller to the agreement. In the same breath he asked me, "What would you like to do?" If I wanted to pursue the contract, he promised to back me up.

I replied that the seller was not a sophisticated gentleman and I though it was the right thing to do to let him out of the agreement. Mike totally agreed.

The seller knew he was on the hook and was very worried about being forced to sell his property or facing possible legal problems. I knew he was sincere about changing his mind.

He was relieved when I told him I would tear up the listing agreement. As a result, real trust built up with the dairyman and he told others about what had happened. I've gotten business because of how I handled the situation and because Mike was willing to back me up and let me do what I felt was right.

This is a wonderful business. You can set your own hours and pattern. Mike Zagaris has been gracious enough to give me the reins to build up a business that fits my personality, which is not to work fast, but consistently and thoroughly. It is almost to the point now where I need to bring in an assistant in order to grow the thing a little more.

Chapter Four

Surround Yourself with Winners

People rise to the level of those with whom they surround themselves. As parents we understand how important it is to influence the selection of our children's playmates when they're small. We're concerned about who their friends are when they're adolescents. I don't know how many times we hear the parent of a troubled kid say, "Johnny just got in with the wrong crowd."

Why do we think things are any different when we're adults?

Those who surround themselves in their professional and personal lives with people who are positive, energetic, honest and vibrant will benefit from those relationships. They will do better and go further. Those who surround themselves with negative people will find it difficult to be unaffected by their presence. Negative mental states are contagious just like the flu or the common cold.

Since so much of what we do in real estate depends on mental attitude, it is critically important for people in our profession to be discerning about the type of people they choose to associate with.

It is possible to learn a lot from observation. As a real estate broker, I have discovered the business health of my organization is significantly enhanced if from time to time very negative people are weeded out, despite the fact they may appear to be productive. No matter how productive they may seem, negative mental attitudes are destructive to those around them—and to the organization as a whole.

The first conscious step for a real estate agent in creating the best environment in which to work—and in surrounding himself or herself with good people—is selection of a broker. It is crucial to find a broker who recognizes real estate agents as valuable customers, treats them with respect and provides them with a good working environment. It is in that environment where agents conduct their professional practice.

A good place to work also means offering a stimulating learning environment. All professionals, whether they are brand new to the business or seasoned veterans, need to be constantly sharpening their skills.

At PMZ Real Estate we are committed to establishing and maintaining those skills through PMZ University, a comprehensive in-house learning and training center. It is a physical place at our facility and a curriculum with complete orientation for new agents and ongoing training for all agents available at no cost every day of the week.

We also conduct stimulating—though not overly long and burdensome—staff meetings with topical educational content.

A broker, through his or her leadership, provides a tone for the office and the company. At some brokerage firms, agents feel they are treated as children or as employees who are ordered about. This can be very demoralizing to people who have made a conscious decision to enter a profession where they believe they will be in charge of their own destinies.

At some companies management creates a "we" and "they" attitude between agents and the administrative support staff. For instance, clerical staff should be there to serve the agents and provide them with valuable services. But at some firms they work grudgingly, treating agents with disdain or disrespect; they view agents as a nuisance rather than as their customers.

Too often agents will initially make the decision about choosing a broker strictly on who is willing to pay them more. They don't understand the real distinguishing feature between brokers isn't their compensation plans but the quality of the working environment they offer. That has everything to do with how the agents perform.

If agents walk into a company where there are negative office politics, infighting and backbiting, those things will all inhibit performance. If there is a healthy environment where colleagues who are positive surround agents and people are upbeat and happy where they work, that will stimulate agents to build successful practices.

In my experience, it is rare to see an agent move from one company to another strictly over money. Frequently people move because they don't feel respected or treated with dignity.

By contrast, my commitment as a broker is based on the notion that agents are among my most valued customers. My entire organization is geared to meeting the needs of agents so they can be free to achieve their goals and objectives.

Agents who are new to the business would be well served to interview a number of agents who work for or were once associated with any broker they are considering. They should find out as much as they can about that company because there are real differences between brokers.

Like a broker, a real estate agent has the responsibility to create his or her own dynamic team. Every agent works with a number of people in related fields. For example, there are escrow officers working with title companies and loan officers who work with mortgage firms. Sometimes clients choose their loan or escrow officers. But agents can have a lot to say about whom to select. It is important to use good judgment in choosing highly talented and responsive people for these roles.

A loan or escrow officer who doesn't know what he or she is doing can kill a transaction. Regardless of how good the real estate agent is, if the deal falls through it is the agent who will be blamed and the client who will be dissatisfied.

Frequently agents pick loan officers or escrow companies based on a superficial assessment of their capabilities. A loan officer, for example, might be friendly and take them out to lunch, but that doesn't mean they will provide a high quality of service. Agents need to talk with others in the industry and obtain information from as many respected professionals about who is honest, skilled and diligent.

Transaction coordinators are persons who assist agents and their clients by coordinating activities during the escrow process. Agents also will hire assistants to work with them in handling the hundreds and thousands of details that need attention.

If there is one area where many agents fall down

it is in not being critical enough in forming a reliable team that can include a loan officer, escrow assistant and transaction coordinator. Agents must be selective and careful in making sure their teams share their sense of ethics, hard work, responsibility, sensitivity and responsiveness to the client.

PMZ Real Estate is a family business founded by my father, Paul M. Zagaris, who started his real estate career in 1947. Before coming west he was a coal miner in Wyoming and a U.S. Army soldier in World War II.

All four of his children eventually joined him in the business. Today it is run by my sister, Paula, my brother, Jon, and myself. Our brother Steve passed away in 2000.

In addition, my brother-in-law, Duke Leffler, works at PMZ and my sister-in-law, Grace Zagaris, works at Qualified Mortgage, our family's home loan company. Now some from the next generation, our children, are also starting in the business. At PMZ we have a deeply felt conviction that families working together comprise a great business model. This is why we encourage agents to bring family members into their teams.

Real estate offers a unique opportunity for families that want to be self-employed to enjoy substantial financial rewards and not be obligated to come up with a large capital investment. For example, if you wish to open a retail store, it requires buying or leasing the building, investing in equipment and furniture, purchasing inventory, hiring employees, deducting and forwarding state and federal taxes, paying for Social Security and workers' compensation and unemployment insurance.

As real estate professionals, family members get

the chance to be compensated well without having to endure all the headaches.

What's more, a genuine synergy can be realized when the people working together are closely related. Everyone contributes to the same pot. The benefits of a practice flow into one family unit and can more easily be shared among the parties without the kind of disputes that can arise when people are unrelated and one person feels he or she is contributing more than someone else.

There is nothing more powerful than a family working together in real estate. My family has worked together and I understand the value of these special relationships. So at PMZ we encourage the participation of people in our company who wish to work with family members.

There are all kinds of different arrangements between families working in this business. At PMZ we have married couples working together, each a strong agent with his or her own book of business—and they cover for each other when necessary. There are couples where one spouse provides support for the other who is more dominant. There are women who take the lead and are backed up by their husbands—and vice versa. There are teams where one spouse's strengths compensate for the weaknesses of the other—and vice versa.

I have seen it a lot and I love it. It is an amazing thing to watch—and it is a trend in our industry.

An individual agent can perform well and build a financially rewarding practice. But at the end of the day a business principally based on personal relationships is not something that can be easily sold to someone else. Clients won't necessarily work with a new agent just because the old agent says so. However, if a son or daughter joins the practice, for example, the agent over time can transfer the relationships that were built up to the child. It is a way to preserve a valuable asset that would otherwise be difficult or impossible to pass on from one generation to the next.

Say an agent who has worked hard over a number of years to establish a lucrative practice wants to start slowing down. The son or daughter can begin covering for the father or mother. The child can come to know and be trusted by the clients. Some day the child can inherit the entire client base from the parent.

Following are a sampling of PMZ agents with stories that supply some examples to consider.

❖

Carla Torkelson: *'Families Add Another Dimension'*

Although 53 when she went into real estate, Carla Torkelson had an extensive background in finance and accounting. She works as part of a team with her husband, Hank.

Born in Spokane, Wash. in 1947, I was raised in nearby Coeur d'Alene, Idaho, my father's hometown, until the age of 13. My family on my father's side were entrepreneurial people, small business owners. My grandparents owned the first drive-in restaurant with carhops in Coeur d'Alene.

It was difficult growing up. I was the oldest of five children. My father was an alcoholic who eventually died of the disease at age 56. My parents divorced when I was eight and my father left. From then on I took care of the younger children while my mother worked.

We were really poor, but you don't really notice when you're a kid. Other things are more important. My grandparents on my father's side helped the best they could. But my mother was mostly on her own.

When I was 13, we moved to North Carolina and lived with mother's parents for a while. I went to high school in North Carolina but came back and graduated in the Northwest while living with my father in Spokane.

I had become pregnant as a senior in high school, where I was head majorette. I didn't tell anyone. The day I graduated in spring 1965, I drove to Seattle, having saved money while working. It was a whole different age. We didn't know about birth control. But I didn't want to get married, which was the norm at the time. And I didn't want to go to a home for unwed mothers. I wanted to remain independent. I had plans for myself. I had always wanted to go to college.

Having put away some money to get through the period when I knew I wouldn't be working, I moved to Seattle, got an apartment and had twins, a boy and a girl. I also went to business school during the summer to learn to use accounting machines.

My first job was at Boeing Aircraft in the computer department. In 1965, and I was into computers. Since I saw people were promoted from within the company, I asked the boss to be considered for computer operator, the next step up for me. "We are promoting from within," he confirmed, "but we're not promoting women." I sent out 100 resumes to banks and insurance companies, looking for a computer operator position.

In 1967, I became the first female computer operator at Seattle First National Bank, working nights and taking less pay than men doing the same job, just to have the opportunity. Women made less money then. That's just the way it was.

In the early 1970s, I moved to Fresno, Calif., where I learned to become a bookkeeper. I knew you could get a free education in California. I later attended a junior college and Cal State Hayward. I ended up receiving my B.S. degree in accounting from the University of San Francisco extension program.

Working full time in accounting and computing while going to college, I also got married to my first husband. I ended up as corporate controller for computer companies in San Ramon, Pleasanton and Livermore, where I raised my kids and eventually got divorced.

After they graduated from high school I moved to Modesto to be able to buy a house. By then I was teaching accounting on the computer in my own business. Over time, I took a position with a computer system integration company and commuted from Modesto to the East Bay for 11 years.

I always loved real estate and had accounting clients and friends in the profession in the East Bay. In 1994, I married Hank. That same year he became a real estate agent and joined PMZ Real Estate. Hank encouraged me join him in the business and I got my license in 2000.

As a businessperson and entrepreneur, right away I was in love with the real estate business. Mike Zagaris encouraged me to go to a four-day training seminar. I became aware that if I wanted a fast-track learning curve—since I wasn't that young anymore—it would be to my benefit to learn systems that were already proven. I signed up for real estate coaching by Mike Ferry's organization, which made all the difference in the world.

My first year in business I completed 31 transactions, which was phenomenal for a first year. The next year I did 51. This year I will probably break 80 transactions.

I already had a vast background in finance and

accounting, having worked very closely with many CEOs and people who ran businesses. I believe I am a good judge of a CEO; I've worked for good ones and bad ones.

Mike is a brilliant guy and a great CEO. He speaks the truth—and he's a very straightforward talker. He's also a big thinker. That doesn't only come to people who are rich or famous. It's an attribute of people who think with a certain mindset.

Growing up I didn't surround myself with big thinkers. I was young and impoverished. Today, I am constantly trying to be around people who are big thinkers. You can have people around you who think big and those who do not. You have to consciously think about it.

One advantage of going into real estate at the age I did was I didn't end up with some fly-by-night outfit. People who are just getting into real estate may go to work for the company where they took courses without thinking about the direction the CEO is taking the company.

As a real estate agent you're on your own. I wake up every day unemployed. Every day my job is to go out and get business. It's not like you wake up, show up for work and receive a salary.

What Mike provides us with is an environment of encouragement. He provides good technology and a great place to work. He has a lot of long-term agents who have done well in the environment he provides. It comes from Mike's mindset of being a visionary and a big thinker. He puts a lot of money into technology and state-of-the-art ideas. Some of them I use; some of them I don't. But the point is he's always attempting to stay on the cutting edge.

Hank and I have two staff members working with us. I tell them this is an adult business. It doesn't matter if you're young or old—it's a hard line of work. You have to be disciplined and consistent. You need to learn to practice and grow. That's the same message Mike sends his agents.

I've never called Mike to ask him to meet with me or talk with me on the phone for advice where he wasn't totally available. But he doesn't tell me I should be doing this or that. He encourages independent thinking. It's the same with the younger or newer agents.

It starts with his hiring process. He's very interested in hiring people with good character. He tries to hire people who won't get him sued and who have the character to do the business well because he wants them to be successful. He provides the environment, but that is not enough. He doesn't want just anyone who can get a license. He wants agents who will put in the time, energy and commitment to the business.

Then he treats them like adults. He offers them training through PMZ University, where I occasionally drop in for inspiration. It's a great opportunity to meet with Mike and other agents who are as committed as you are. It's great training at our office and at no expense.

I have a lot of clients who are single women I am trying to help get into housing. It's tremendously difficult when they're alone and single to figure out how to get things done. Most can only afford houses that need a lot of work. So they buy and end up having to paint rooms or get the heater fixed when it goes out. A lot of times they are ill-equipped and need us to serve as a resource.

So I've found when a husband and wife work as a team, that creates a synergy that is very powerful. Because there are two of us, my husband, Hank, and I, when we encounter problems or set goals or have decisions to make, we can figure out a direction to take. Working with other people creates an environment of mutual encouragement and support.

Since I'm now 57, I want to figure out who's successful and copy that success rather than reinventing it. So I study the high producing agents. I notice the majority of those people who are highly successful have family members in their business with them. Husbands and wives. Children. Brothers. Sisters.

What makes it better is that as family they seem as committed to your success as their own. They are not likely to tell other agents about your strategies and techniques. This is a highly competitive business. I'd love to compete with other agents for listings. I practice being good at what I do so I can get them. It's not that I'm looking for the business of my colleagues. I'm looking for any business and to be as good as the best in my craft.

Family adds another dimension to the business. It gives them a place to go. If an agent is aging, a younger family member can become more involved. It's the same reason family-owned businesses bring family members into their stores or restaurants. You have a certain level of trust or they wouldn't be there with you.

I'm blessed to have a great team, but other than my husband, I don't have family members nearby. I want to do 200 deals a year by the end of 2006. That's why I have a terrific staff.

❖

DENNIS LILLY: *'A Synergy For Success'*

Dennis works with his wife, Nancy, plus his sons, Zach and Jarod, his sister, Lona Lilly Davis, and lifetime friend and business associate, Derek Wood.

I was born in Oakdale in 1955 and grew up in Modesto. My mother was a homemaker. My father worked three jobs at the same time: elected county clerk of Stanislaus County, accountant for Sears and manager of a music band.

After Downey High School I attended Modesto Junior College. I met my wife at age 16. As soon as I graduated from the junior college I joined the Army and got married—all at 19. I went to college at night while I was in the Army and stationed at Ford Ord. While in the service I had a small house painting and janitorial business. I graduated with a B.S. degree in organizational management from the University of San Francisco after I returned to Modesto to raise a family. My wife, Nancy, obtained her nursing degree at the same time.

I always enjoyed retail sales, having taken courses in high school. I always liked selling services and continued house painting and janitorial management after moving to Modesto on my days off while working for Rainbo Bakery.

I drove a truck for 10 years, selling bread products around the county. There were great people in that business but miserable working conditions with days going more than 12 hours.

In 1987, I started taking classes in real estate principles and got my license in 1988. I worked part time in real estate sales and then retired from the truck driving route sales job and went to work full time in real estate starting in 1989.

I started in residential and ranch sales at Prudential California Realty. I did really well. I was rookie of the year at the company and among the top in sales six or seven out of the ten or eleven years I was there. I brought my wife in to work with me as my assistant eight years ago. She got her license and we became a team.

We left for PMZ in 1998. The broker I was with was a wonderful guy with a good vision. But his company was slow in moving towards his annual goals. Nothing was really happening as projected.

I watched Mike Zagaris on the other hand establish a good three-, four- and five-year plan on where he wanted to go—and he was accomplishing it.

Mike talked with us for about six weeks before we made the move. My wife, Nancy, Derek Wood (another agent who grew up with me), our lender, Mary Niles, and I all moved together to PMZ and we continue to work as a team.

At PMZ, we initially lost some business from clients who could no longer find us. Eventually we got the business back with hard work and smart marketing. We were doing about $11 million at Prudential when we left. At PMZ, we've been at $27 million to $30 million the last three years. We've been among the top three agents at the company three out of the last six years in volume of units and dollar closings.

Last year I brought in my sister, Lona Lilly Davis, as an agent to assist us with our sales and clients. Also joining us as an agent is our son, Zach, who graduated from Sacramento State with a degree in business and a minor in real estate. Now we have five agents plus Mary, the lender. We call ourselves the Lilly Group.

The business model we follow is how the Zagaris family has worked together to build a wonderful company, highly recognized in the real estate industry. As a family we've always worked hard and stayed in close contact. Because of our growth and success, other family members have become attracted to the business. My son loves working together as a family in a real estate career.

As a nurse, my wife, Nancy, definitely knows how to multi-task. She makes a great office manager, assisting with listing management, coordinating transactions through escrow and now acting as our team coach. This increases our ability to close escrows—and make sure they do close. We have a very low escrow fallout rate; very few of our deals ever fall out of escrow.

Our level of synergy comes from the excitement and fun of working together, being creative, bouncing ideas off each other, exploring different techniques of marketing—and deciding which are more effective for our clients. Up to 42 people can touch a single escrow in some way. When a crisis happens, we decide how to correct the problem—and what can be done to make the process smoother and more effective.

Because of our known ability to close escrows, agents we work with are more receptive to accepting our clients' offers because they know we have a reputation for closing escrows and making things happen so there's a win-win-win-win situation for the buyer, the seller, the buyer's agent and the listing agent.

Someone is always available for our clients. If one of us is out of town, someone else is there to help. Our clients never feel abandoned. They rely on us for information and to get results. When the client runs into problems, especially during the negotiating and escrow process, an agent can't all of a sudden be missing. Everything is built on timeliness and service.

In today's market, we're lacking on inventory. Agents have to be constantly aware of properties that are coming on the market. Instead of one agent looking around for properties or buyers, we have two, three or four agents looking. If one of us sees a property that is suddenly available and might fit the needs of one of our clients, that person brings it up right away. Then we have a greater chance of getting an offer accepted before multiple offers hit the table.

We try to build a reputation so people know we're available to our clients and also other agents in the transaction as well as the escrow officers, lenders and inspectors. Everyone else in the transaction has to be taken care of. So we need to make sure our clients' needs and everyone else's needs are being met. That's important to us.

All this produces a great environment and a synergy for success in the transaction and for future transactions too. We get a lot of respect and referrals from past clients. It's not just about us; it's about meeting the needs of our clients and colleagues in the business.

I have found myself gravitating towards successful people I've met—from teachers, coaches and military personnel to current colleagues—because they've been there and experienced both success and failure. Those who succeed come out of setbacks with the attitude that they've learned lessons.

Mike has had many great successes—and a few failures from the past that he is more than willing to share with you. He's the kind of guy who bounces back, constantly thinks of new things and makes them work. He's a pure joy to talk with and be around to explore new possibilities on how both agents and the company can market themselves. He loves to hear and embrace new ideas.

Because he sees his agents as his clients and he very much wants his agents to be successful, Mike gives us the tools we need to sell and be productive. He counsels us on life insurance, personal financing, budgeting—however he might be able to help us benefit from his knowledge and experience. He will talk individually with each and every one of us at the company.

The tools he provides so we can be successful in taking care of our clients range anywhere form state-of-the-art Internet features to quality advertising and signage to well-trained and service-oriented staff. There are great classes continuously offered at PMZ University. He encourages successful agents to teach the newer agents about everything from how to conduct a successful open house to time management to how to handle floor calls (people calling into the office for information on a property) to how to handle questions and answers during a presentation (I've given some of those classes before).

A number of brokers throughout the industry say they treat agents like clients so they can better take care of their clients. But Mike adheres to that commitment to the T. He has never wavered from it. That's one reason why I work with this company. I also like the way the Zagaris family operates. If they say they're going to do something, they do it. They do it well. And they're there for you.

I've been at companies where the staff is good, but not up to the level of quality you would expect at a multi-million dollar company. At PMZ, agents really depend on the staff's reliability and commitment at a level of energy that is professional. PMZ has a great staff that has been around, understands the process and assists the agents above and beyond.

In choosing ancillary personnel, you need people with in-depth knowledge who understand that service to clients is king. The lender I use has been in the business for 25 years. She has owned her own company and has managed different mortgage firms. She has a can-do attitude that matches mine. We have not failed any buyer. She pre-qualifies buyers and takes them through the end of escrow. She knows where to take loans to get what buyers would like to have. She acts like the offensive coordinator of a professional football team. It's great to watch her in action.

When you call up and talk with an escrow officer about a client, you need that person to have knowledge of the escrow and its timing even though it is one of many escrows the officer is handling at that time. There are many escrow officers in this community. The ones I use are on top of items in escrow all the time. They are very professional and service oriented with an emphasis on the needs of the client. And management solidly backs them up.

By the way, our youngest son, Jarod, graduated from UC Berkeley with a degree in political science. He has been working for a title company for the past three years in Berkeley and is now full time in Modesto. Jarod is now going to be managing our property acquisition company with my son Zach as part of the Lilly Group. We will always have a bias towards working together as a family.

❖

CHRIS SHAW:
PMZ Really Does Treat Agents Like Customers

For more of Chris Shaw's story see Chapter Two.

When Mike Zagaris talks about treating the Realtors® as customers, that is a very unique attitude—and practice. Most brokers look at agents as quasi-employees there to provide income to the company.

Mike looks at us as if we are his customers, just as our buyers and sellers are our customers. So in essence, he serves us. Other brokerage companies provide services to agents to assure the companies' success. There is a subtle but important difference. I didn't perceive it initially. Then, after a period of time with

PMZ, I saw changes being made. We were already the number one real estate company, yet additional services were being provided to the Realtors®. I realized how important it is to Mike to serve us.

For instance, senior agents, including Mike, provide some of the training. He taps agents in the company with particular expertise in certain areas and invites them to share their knowledge with other agents. It's really a good situation when you can actually learn from other people in the company who are more successful than you are and who are right there in the trenches next to you being exposed to the same conditions.

One of the gripes I have with professional real estate trainers is they talk about how things are in the Midwest, Florida or Los Angeles. That doesn't really have much bearing on what I do here. If I can learn from an agent right here doing exactly what I'm doing who is more experienced and successful than I am, that's extremely valuable and very relevant.

I have had an assistant and a transaction coordinator for about three years. I look for people who are positive thinkers and possess skills that are not my strengths. For example, my assistant is strong with computers where I'm not. My transaction coordinator is very detail oriented, thorough and even-tempered. Since I've hired these people and joined forces with them, my income has gone way up, mostly due to two reasons: They free me up to focus on what I do best, which is to list and sell. And both of these people are more skilled at what they do than when I attempted to handle those tasks on my own.

I also used to find it very frustrating to work on the tasks they now handle, especially the escrow process that the transaction coordinator does. I used to work hard all morning on a particularly difficult escrow and then have to hop in my car and try to be in a good frame of mind when I was trying to list or sell in the afternoon. It was tough to be on top of my game.

Now the instructions to my staff are for them to handle the problems until they hit a roadblock, and then bring it to me. They're able to handle most things. It's definitely money well spent if you have the right people.

It's the same thing when you work with a lender. The lender can make your life much simpler by working only with qualified prospective buyers. When they're representing buyers, young agents will work with people who can't afford to purchase or who want to purchase what they can't afford. A good lender will quickly screen out those who won't qualify.

❖

KEVIN BORDEN: *'PMZ Opens the Door'*

He has helped build up a successful real estate business with his family, which employs some proactive marketing strategies.

My dad was a sales rep for a furniture manufacturer in Louisville, Ky., where I was born in 1972. Then we moved to Minnesota. My whole family on my dad's side was in real estate there. We moved to Sunnyvale, Calif. when I was seven. In my second year in high school we moved to Modesto and have been here ever since.

When the kindergarten teacher asked the kids what we wanted to be when we grew up, I would always say "real estate." After two years at California State University, Stanislaus, I finally went to my parents and told them I wanted to get into this business and live my dream; I wanted to sink or swim in the real world.

I swam.

In 1993, I got a job as an assistant to a local Realtor® at Re/Max in Modesto. I wanted a taste of the business to find out what it was all about. I did everything to support him so he could be out on appointments building his business and making money. I placed calls to clients and handled all the escrow coordinating and mailings.

It went great. Then I got cocky. I was a young kid and wanted more money. He couldn't support me. My dad, David Borden, had been in real estate since 1988. I went to him and proposed that we do a father-and-son operation.

So we went into business at Prudential. Our somewhat cheesy slogan was, "Father and son sold another."

Two years into the business, my mom, Janet, was laid off from her job and she came over to be with us too. Then I met my soon-to-be-wife, Janette, and my dad hired her.

We were starting out brand new, but the market was tanking as we got into it. Because of the times, we had to get really creative. We staged community seminars: How to buy a HUD home. How to buy and sell a home.

The idea was we would share our knowledge with the community with an open hand. We were able to meet people and they could see how we work and have the opportunity to work with us. These seminars were very successful and we still do them. We've offered the classes at local libraries, at high schools for students' parents and at Modesto Junior College as a continuing education course.

From Prudential, we met with Mike Zagaris and several other brokers in town. We decided Mike had the foresight and the same big picture thinking we did. His whole goal is to give us the tools so we can be successful in a way that doesn't nickel and dime us. At Prudential they started charging us for things other brokers took care of, and they focused on new agents. PMZ also takes on new agents and trains them; however, Mike also makes sure the successful agents stay successful.

Since coming to PMZ in 1998, it has been awesome. Even during personal trials, like when my dad had heart surgery in 2002, we continued to do well. Mike gave us time to get through that and he has given us what we needed to continue.

Our business just keeps growing and growing. We've always worked to take care of our current and past clients and to keep in touch with them. We've made a new commitment to focus on past clients through an impressive database, communicating with them at least once a month.

We've implemented our "pop by" program, just a little thing to show how much we appreciate our clients. We took someone else's idea and ran with it.

Clients who provide referrals on an ongoing basis get hit every month with a pop by gift; for those who do business with us or give us one referral, we come by and deliver the pop by every quarter. This month's gift is a baggy with half a pound of almonds. On the back we include a little recipe.

Every month we'll hit our clients with a client appreciation program item. In November, around Thanksgiving, we give a colored sheet of paper explaining the meaning of the holiday and its origins plus ideas for games families can play around the dinner table. There is also a coupon worth 15 percent off for a company that supplies gift baskets featuring customized nuts.

When the postal service changes stamps, we send all our clients 10 one-cent stamps with a little note saying, "Hey, we thought you might need these." People get stuck with old stamps they can't use anymore.

The whole point of these efforts with our clients is to show them we're competent and they're important to us. Without them we would not have a business. The gifts keep us in their remembrance so when they encounter someone who wants to buy or sell, they refer them to us.

It works. Since beginning this in May 2004, we've had an extraordinary increase in referrals. In October alone we received five referrals where we listed or sold a house. We used to get them before, but not on such a regular basis.

We're at PMZ because Mike respects us as individual agents and encourages us to go out and be successful at our own level. He gives us the tools to do it. Take PMZ.com with its "What is Happening in Your Neighborhood" service. I punch in a client's name, address, phone number and email address. Automatically, when a property changes status or becomes active—a new active listing or a pending sale—my client is emailed with information. The service constantly updates clients and continues to let them know what is happening in their neighborhood. The client also sees a picture of me every time they receive something from PMZ online.

There is also the "Buyer Instant Notification" online at PMZ. If a client is a buyer I put him or her into the computer with an email address. As soon as a property comes on the market that fits that client's criteria, the system automatically emails information to the person on that property. And I come up as the agent sending it.

It's a seller's market. This system gives my clients a better chance to get to a new property first. They don't have to wait for me to call them. It's there. Then they can call me to say they want to go see that house. It's a great tool.

Ads are also placed online. I get on the PMZ website, type in my ad, save it and it automatically downloads to the Modesto Bee.

All lawn signs are also web-based. I log on the website, type in the address where I want the sign to go up, hit send and if it's before noon someone goes out within a day to put up the lawn sign. It's streamlined.

Then Mike has PMZ University. Here is a guy who runs extremely successful businesses, yet he devotes time every Monday morning to brainstorm with whoever wants to show up. We brainstorm about ideas that work and those that don't. He'll usually bring a topic. One time it was time management, making time work for you. He'll offer ideas on how he uses his time. He also brings in guests. A home warranty company came in to teach agents about what to do to reduce the risks of lawsuits.

Every day of the week there are classes on numerous subjects. We just got a new contract form at PMZ. So there was a class on how to use contracts and what to look out for. New agents get a week of new agent orientation with lunch provided. They learn everything they need to know to start off—what to do, where to go for help. No other company in the area does this so far as I know.

These are just some examples of Mike's commitment to make people successful. He won't do the work for you, but he'll provide what you need to achieve success.

One of those tools is branding. It is hugely important. When I go out to listing appointments, even if they are referrals, I always ask clients if they have any questions about my company or me. "Absolutely not," is a typical answer, "you don't need to tell me anything about PMZ. They're the best out there. I definitely want to list with PMZ."

PMZ opens the door. Clients are already comfortable with PMZ because of its market presence—all the listing and sold signs they see. We're dominant in this market by far.

An extremely powerful real estate tool can be families working together. It's powerful for us because we're not just one person out there trying to make our way. We're a family that knows each other intimately. We each have strengths and weaknesses. We utilize our strengths to cover each other's weaknesses.

It can be even more powerful for the client. An example is when my dad took our daughter to Disneyland and was gone for a week. Business didn't stop. I was still here. My wife, Janette, was still here. And so was Aaron Sauer, my partner and buyer specialist. We didn't lose a step. We even sold a couple of houses while my dad was away. Then Aaron took off with his wife for a vacation to Mexico. Business still ran. If my wife and I are gone, Aaron and my dad are here. We always have coverage. The name of our group is called the Borden Family.

My dad and I still work together, although now he's semi-retired. My wife and mom are still very much a part of the business. We just hired another buyer specialist to help take care of all our buyers.

No one person can always be up. It helps when you have someone next to you who is up when you're down. You feed off each other's energy. There is a synergy to working with people who are related and committed to succeed in business and in the relationships that make families work.

If I were to start all over again in real estate, I

would handle referrals differently. We didn't think of our referral campaign until recently. Without expecting anything, we just took care of our clients. If I was suggesting something to someone just getting into the business it would be to write down the names of everyone they know, who knows them, who they like and love—and call each one of them or stop by and see them. Ask them if they are working with a Realtor®. If they're not, ask if they can be that Realtor®; ask to prove to them that they can take care of people that would be sent their way.

Begin a database that way. Then start by taking care of the clients, being in their lives, doing the extra special things for them that make a difference. By building really good friendships with people it will help your business too.

If I knew those things 10 years ago, I'd be retired by now.

❖

TERRI WESTERN: *Family Members Compliment Each Other*

She is in business with her husband, Grant, and their daughters, Sheri Frey and Stacey Boyers.

I was born in Modesto in 1948. My mother, who is now 89, is a retired accountant. We decided to have her come live with us instead of putting her in a care facility.

My father owned his own meat market in the town of Newman, west of Modesto. We moved around, to San Jose and then Torrance, where I graduated from high school and attended Cerritos Junior College. My goal was to become a dental hygienist because that's the direction I was pointed in by high school aptitude tests, although my interests were in art and design.

My first husband was drafted into the Army and sent to Vietnam with the 101st Airborne Division. I was forced to drop out of college since we had obligations to meet. I worked for Magnavox Corp., in TV and stereo equipment sales.

We moved back to Modesto in 1969, and I went to work in the title department of Title Insurance and Trust Co. I worked my way up to the escrow department. Then I learned I loved doing outside sales more. I took a job with the Holt-Hartmon & Co. mortgage firm. I stayed in the mortgage business. My last position was area manager for a joint venture of Norwest Mortgage and Wells Fargo Bank, covering half the state, from Visalia north to Redding.

I had been a single mother for 12 years while raising my two daughters. Grant and I married in 1993 when I was managing mortgage companies and handling loans for his clients. He was an agent with PMZ.

When the kids became young adults, I didn't want to labor at such a stressful job that required a lot of traveling. By 1997, when Wells Fargo and Norwest dissolved their joint venture, I was tired of the big corporate world dictating my future. I thought to myself: I'm a type A personality who wants to be the driver of my own bus. So I decided to join Grant in selling real estate. It was an easy transition since I had managed mortgage companies and understood all the different kinds of loans that matched different types of clients and properties.

For instance, if I do a market evaluation for a home with asbestos shingle siding, which a lot of older homes have, I know that home could not be sold with FHA mortgage financing. Each lending entity—such as Fannie Mae, Freddie Mac, VA and FHA—has its own definitive rules and regulations.

So knowing the title, escrow and lending sides and having full knowledge of all the available kinds of loans made it an easy transition. Plus, I was joining Grant, who already had a book of business because he had been in real estate since 1988.

I tapped a lot of the sources I had developed over the years—all my past clients—in building my real estate business. I kept in touch with them through a database.

Over the years we grew and expanded to the point where the two of us weren't enough. So we recently brought my youngest daughter, Stacey Boyers, into our business. She passed her test and works with us as an agent. She comes to the table with knowledge of things Grant and I are relatively slow at: the technology end of things. We learned to use computers for the functions we need. But Stacey is very knowledgeable with computers. She is able to take care of a lot of the advertising and production of fliers and posters that we used to have to pay to have done. She's also very good at marketing. We call our business the Western Group.

Before Stacey joined us, we brought on our oldest daughter, Sheri Frey, as an assistant to Grant and me in 2001. Sheri decided she wanted to coordinate for a lot of other agents too. She now works for six other agents, doing transaction coordinating at PMZ's Carpenter Road office. She also still does work for us.

All of us in the Western Group are different people when it comes to energy and knowledge. Grant's strengths are my weaknesses and my strengths are his weaknesses. I'm more of a people person. My primary job is to bring in business. I get involved in quite a few things. I'm out playing golf or participating in fundraising for some worthy cause where I meet a lot of people. Grant is excellent at research—the ability to sit in front of a computer at a desk and do evaluations.

While we're different, we compliment each other. That's why we're so successful. Stacey brings in a new breath of fresh air. She joined an organization called the Central Valley Professional Exchange, a group of young executive types that meets once a month, does a lot for the community and helps members get started in their own fields. They range from bankers to business owners to marketing and professional people. Stacey is already getting real estate leads from her involvement with that group.

Grant and I are both 56 years old. We're not in touch with younger people. Stacey brings us sellers and buyers from that age group whom we wouldn't normally come in contact with. She has worked out well because Stacey doesn't have to worry that clients will wonder if she knows what she's doing since she is a new agent who just got her license. We go with her when she does a market evaluation or presentation to a buyer, which gives her the credibility of having experience on her side. If clients are interviewing agents, either to list or buy homes, they know experience is invaluable.

I love being around people of all different types, young and old. All my daughter's friends who grew up at our house still come around. I feel no matter how old I become chronologically, mentally I'm still young at heart. Being around younger people keeps me that way.

My daughter, Stacey, and Lacy Rocha Peterson grew up together. They were like sisters since the third grade. Lacy grew up at my house.

When I received the call from Stacey on that Christmas Eve about Lacy being missing, it was the kind of call no parent ever wants to receive. I was at their home the day after Christmas when 50 or 60 people were lined up out the front door to pick up fliers and help in the search. I talked with the manager of the Red Lion Hotel and explained what we needed. He set us up with a place where all of the girls and the entire Modesto community came together—and where the press congregated.

People who didn't even know Lacy offered money, supplies, computers, copy machines—whatever we needed. A bagel shop and pizza parlor brought in food.

All those management skills I developed came into play. I helped set things up at the Red Lion and communicate with the media. We got different people to take charge of various areas. A ton of talent turned out to help. The community served Lacy's family very well during that tragedy.

When I was at it 24/7, Grant would come down to the Red Lion at 10 p.m. after I had been there since 7:30 in the morning and he would tap on his wristwatch.

Now I spend time with our grandson, Tyler, and enjoy going with him to the park. I'm able to work a lot of hours at this job—pretty much 24/7. But my job still gives me the ability to take off maybe two hours during the day, pick up my grandson from school or visit the pumpkin patch or the Christmas tree lot with him. I am better able to do that with Tyler than I was with my children as a single parent managing mortgage companies.

I can still work hard and play too. It's also important for mental health and physical well-being.

Grant and I have the opportunity to go to work for any brokerage agency in this town, maybe because they follow the stats and know we do big volume and are good agents. Speaking from the heart, I don't think anyone could offer us any amount of money to change companies. I wouldn't move from PMZ.

Mike gives us all the tools we need to be the best we can be. Shame on us if we don't use them.

The man is always on the cutting edge of the next best tool that keeps us in the know—from knowledge of what's happening in the marketplace to having an IT staff that helps us with all of our computer needs. We have without a doubt the best website, bar none. Other brokers have their agents use our PMZ website because it's so good. Those agents will tell their clients who want to buy a home to go to PMZ's website to look around. It's very user friendly, up to date and accurate.

Some national websites like Homefinders.com are out there. But often they have old inventory. That's why a lot of folks use our website even though they're not using us as agents. It's quite a compliment to Mike, his forethought and the IT people he hires.

Driving through Modesto, you will see more PMZ signs than anything else, no doubt. That's a big plus too. So is the advertising PMZ does in newspapers, on the radio and the Internet. Where else can you get that?

If you work for companies like Re/Max, Coldwell Banker, Prudential or Century 21, part of the split out of every commission goes to pay the franchise fee. Different companies use different methods. We don't do that at PMZ. Yet we get so much more as agents.

PMZ's advertising dollars get spent locally and people pay attention to the ads. Mike's involvement in advertising and the community helps us tremendously. He started out as a boutique company his father started. I remember in the '60s, when Paul Zagaris, Mike's father, brought escrows to us when I was in the title business. They were one-page contracts. Now it practically takes a whole tree to put together a deal.

Grant and I are so loyal to PMZ because it is like working for a family. Even though they've grown this big, you always feel like you're in a comfort zone at PMZ. Mike will be passing through the office or I can be walking out to the car in the parking lot and he will call across and say hi and take time to pay attention to you.

Chapter Five

Build Your Own Personal Brand

A chief factor influencing where buyers and sellers turn for professional real estate services is whether they are attracted to a company because its brand name is perceived as being effective and powerful.

This draw is so significant that thousands of real estate companies owned by small business people enter into franchise arrangements with firms that boast brand name recognition. These small operators pay very substantial fees for the right to use the brand name.

At PMZ, we've developed an independent brand that has become the best-known name in the markets where we operate. Awareness studies conducted by an independent research firm have asked residents in PMZ's market area which brand name comes to mind when they think about real estate. PMZ is number one in our market by a large margin.

A brand name is genuinely important for the simple reason that people are drawn to it.

If an independent real estate company possesses

a market dominant brand it has a major advantage since the money that would otherwise go to pay for building brand recognition through a franchise agreement with a national company could be deployed locally for advertising and marketing in support of local agents.

If a brokerage office connected with a franchise firm receives a $10,000 commission on a sale, part of that amount, perhaps $600, has to be sent off to the far-away national franchisor as payment for use of its name. At PMZ, we apply that money locally to fund advertising and other forms of assistance benefiting our agents and don't have to charge our agents any franchise fees.

In a franchise arrangement, three parties share in the proceeds: the agent, broker and franchisor. With an independent real estate company such as PMZ there are only two: the agent and the broker.

The independent firm is the better business model if that broker has dominant brand recognition. It's an inferior model if the broker has little or no name recognition.

In selecting a real estate company with which to work, agents should be mindful of its power in the marketplace where they are attempting to build their practices.

At PMZ Real Estate, we also recognize the importance of each agent developing and cultivating his or her own personal brand. In so doing an agent creates added perceived value to his or her services.

Agents face a dual requirement, a combination of creating a brand and then marketing that brand on a limited budget.

As important as it is for each agent to create and build a personal brand, far too many of them spend too much money on self-promotion and activities I can only characterize as vanity advertising. They need to be extremely intelligent and judicious in their allocation of their limited resources in marketing themselves.

Following are just five PMZ Real Estate agents who discuss the role of brand recognition for both the broker and the agent.

❖

Ron Feldhaus: *'Leaders in Branding as Agents'*

Ron and his son, Randy, are both strong agents at PMZ.

I was born in 1950 and raised in the Bay Area, where my dad was a house painter and my mom stayed at home. I went to work in service stations right out of high school in San Leandro. By age 20, I was too young to have a franchise on my own. So I was into business with a partner who officially owned a Union 76 station in San Leandro.

I realized working 14 hours a day seven days a week wasn't worth the money I was making. So I bought a Snap-on tool franchise business, owning a truck that sold tools to all the mechanics in my area.

From there I went into the automotive repair book business in Los Angeles, selling manuals to mechanics and auto body shops detailing specifications for every kind of repair. My wife and I moved back to San Leandro and ran an antique store in Oakland for seven years. In 1982, we went broke in the restaurant business after moving to Modesto.

By 1983, at 32 years of age, I had known success as a young man who once had plenty of money. Now I had no money. What could I do? Go sell real estate, I thought. I took a class in real estate, got my license and worked for 15 years with a small local real estate company that became a Prudential franchise.

The first few years were a struggle as the business grew slowly. I didn't know what I was doing. There wasn't a lot of training like there is today. I didn't make any money the first couple of years.

My wife, Carol, joined me as an agent in 1986 and we worked together as a team. She retired for health reasons in 2002.

I started attending seminars, learning new strategies and marketing ideas—and learning how to promote myself, search for clients and better run the business.

Things were changing at Prudential. It is a good company, but its goals were different than mine. Being in the business all those years in the same city, I knew Mike Zagaris fairly well. We had conversations over the years. He contacted me and asked if I wanted to talk. My wife and I came to PMZ in 1998. Our son, Randy, came to work with us in 2000.

My business was already good when I came to PMZ. But it definitely improved after I got here. One thing that is different for agents at PMZ are the many tools at our disposal and all the efforts that are made to take pressure off of us at the office so we can go out and sell and do what we have to do.

I think it's important for the average agent to be able to go out and talk with clients and potential clients about the volume of business we do compared to the competition. The difference is so big that there is no comparison.

That kind of branding gets you in the door. Agents are able to field floor calls and it does provide business for them at PMZ because people are calling in.

I choose not to participate in opportunity time, so I do not receive the benefit. But when I'm out trying to convince someone to list his or her home with me, it gives me a distinct advantage to be from PMZ.

We are also leaders in branding as agents. If you are going to sell your house, call PMZ and don't know anyone special, you'll get whomever answers the phone. If you know Ron and Randy Feldhaus from our advertising or because of a referral from a friend or relative, the business comes to us. That's why we began advertising by hiring a marketing person back in 1989 or '90.

He took a lot of photographs and put together a brochure. We ran ads in the newspaper. In those days we were among the first real estate professionals placing ads. Not many Realtors® were advertising then. There are a lot of them doing it now.

For a long time, my wife and I used the slogan "Ron and Carol Feldhaus, the Power of Two" in every newspaper ad, on all our business cards and letterhead. People all over town, in both the real estate and general communities, knew who the Power of Two was from our advertising and promotions. It worked very well for us, separating us from a lot of the competition at the time.

When our son joined our practice about five years ago we moved to the slogan "Ron, Randy and Carol Feldhaus, the Power of Three." After my wife retired we completely changed over to a new slogan. Now everything we do says, "Ron and Randy Feldhaus, Experience Spanning Generations."

What does all this branding do? When we meet with someone we have never seen before, he or she has likely seen our picture in the paper for years. It's like the person already knows us and feels more comfortable doing business.

We'll be in restaurants or movie theaters and people come up and talk with us: "You're the Feldhauses, we see your picture in the paper. You sell real estate."

Most of the time people have questions about how the market is doing or they like to tell horror stories of unpleasant experiences. When it comes time to need a Realtor®, they'll turn to us

We don't advertise as heavily as we used to. Over the years we have acquired a referral base that doesn't require us to use ads as much as we once did. We worked our system by advertising—spending money to get our name out there.

My son has a different approach. He picks up the phone and calls past clients plus friends and acquaintances to keep in touch and generate a lot of referrals.

Still, branding has been good to us. There is no question we were in it early enough and got our name out there so much that our approach has treated us well. We have spent a fair amount of money doing it because ads in newspapers aren't cheap—and we hired a graphic designer to do it right: controlling the photo shoots, placing ads, putting brochures together, producing the business cards, letterheads and envelopes. Everything people get or see from me has my picture and name along with PMZ's logo. But we're dominant.

❖

GEORGIA BILYEU: *'Georgia on My Mind'*

She has become known far and wide by her slogan, "Georgia on my mind."

I was born in a small town just north of Forsyth, Missouri, where we lived until I was five. Then my parents moved to California and I grew up in Modesto.

After Oakdale High School, I went to beauty college and became a hairdresser for five years. I developed an allergy to the chemicals so I went to a local business college to brush up on my secretarial skills. After two weeks I started working afternoons part time after school in a real estate office.

After four years I went to work for Title Insurance and Trust Co. as an escrow secretary, left there and worked in the advertising department of the Modesto Bee. I started out taking ads over the phone on a manual typewriter in the 1970s. Then they moved me onto the outside sales staff. After seven years I was hired back at the title company as business development manager, calling on real estate agents.

After marrying a CPA, having a son and divorcing, I worked for the Stockton Record in outside sales, covering south county, Modesto and Tracy. I worked three and a half years putting 100 miles a day on my car.

I always knew I wanted to be a Realtor®, but I needed to do other things in-between. I thought: I'm smart; I could pass the real estate test. I took a six-day crash course, took and passed the exam and got my license in 1989.

Then I started selling real estate. The first house I sold was my mom and dad's house. For two and a half years I sold real estate—mostly second or recreational homes—at Lake Tullock, a resort community about 45 miles from Modesto in the Sierra foothills, and got married again.

When the phones stopped ringing during Desert Storm, we decided to sell real estate back in Modesto. While working for another broker, I visited an open house for a PMZ agent and asked whether PMZ ever hired agents who were fairly new to the business. By that time I had been selling for about four years. The next thing I knew Phillip Levin, the sales manager at PMZ's Orangeburg office, was calling me. I interviewed with him and Mike Zagaris and came on in 1994.

During the first four or five years at PMZ I averaged about $4 million a year in sales. Since the market picked up, things have gotten better and better each year. By late 2004, with the year still not yet over, I was already at $10 million in volume.

Because I was in advertising so many years at the newspapers, I know you have to set yourself apart from all the other people who also advertise. Success doesn't just come from advertising, but the advertising promotes it. If I have both my referral base and my advertising working together, they complement each other.

I have my own brand recognition. It came about one day when I was brainstorming with a past boss from the Stockton Record. She had been in advertising longer than I had.

"I need a slogan, a representation of who I am," I said.

She laughed and replied, "You have a natural one: 'Georgia on your mind.'"

Right away I put "Georgia on my mind" on my fliers and ran the slogan on my lawn signs. I use it in my ads in the Modesto Bee and frequently in the regional real estate book.

I used a photo that a client took of me after I sold her parents' home. I was nailing up a "sold" sign on top of my lawn sign. She said, "Hold it just a minute—I want to take your picture doing that." She took it and sent it to me. That was 10 years ago. (Now I use a similar photo that has been updated so people can recognize me.)

People call me up because they see or remember the slogan. They often call me right from the lawn sign itself.

"I saw your ad in the paper," they'll say. Or "I saw

your sign."

They just laugh when I answer, "You can remember me, I'm Georgia on your mind."

When I put calls into my clients I always start out by saying, "You've been on my mind"—because it's true.

The slogan and all the interplay it generates set the tone for the conversation. I really am happy to talk with them. The conversation itself can be a progress report for a client. Or they're calling because they want me to help them with their transaction.

Whatever way it goes or whomever I'm talking with it produces laughter, which is a great way to begin. It eases the tension that naturally exists in a transaction. For all of us this is the major purchase of our lifetime and there is a lot of anxiety associated with it. If clients know their agent is in control and they're laughing with her, it takes the edge off. It gives clients the confidence things will work out and everything will be fine. They know they have an ally in me and that we will do this together. I'm not boring. I'm fun and I'm going to guide them safely through the process.

The slogan goes on my fliers, at the property site, in my newspaper ads and in display ads that picture the house.

Where most agents use these advertising and marketing tools to communicate, "This is Georgia Bilyeu, you can reach me here," I'm saying, "Keep Georgia on your mind when you're buying and selling real estate."

I don't use my last name. No one can pronounce it anyway.

❖

LANE MENEZES: 'THE RANCH REALTOR®'

Lane Menezes is known by his slogan "The Ranch Realtor®" because he specializes in selling agricultural properties. To hear more from Lane, read Chapter Three.

My clientele is not pulled into my business by PMZ because it is so specialized. It's me they call, not PMZ. That said, Mike Zagaris gives me incredible insight that could never be purchased from a man with his kind of background and knowledge. And he has been more than generous in sharing information that helps me structure my business—which, in turn, makes me more valuable to my clients.

The ag real estate business deals with people who have a certain lifestyle. It is not residential real estate; it's not ranchettes or commercial real estate. It is its own entity that stands by itself. The people in the business are very unique too.

The Central Valley, from south of Bakersfield to Stockton and Sacramento, feeds the world. We grow everything on this piece of land. The people who own that land are valuable and in a class by themselves. You have to approach each one of them with that in mind.

When you walk up to them, they have to know who you are. If they don't, they won't give you the time of day.

To do that it takes being consistent, having integrity and telling it like it is, good or bad. You have to have it in your heart; it must be within you.

It's easy to tell clients what they want to hear so they don't get angry with you. You can't do that in the ag land business. You have to tell them the truth whether it makes them mad or not. If you tell a farmer the truth, he'll deal with it. He may not like it, but he'll deal with it.

Maybe it's something in the contract that has to be changed because there were more costs than the buyer anticipated. Or there are more costs than the seller had thought and the buyer has to come up with more money.

The good thing is that 80 or 85 percent of the time I am the agent representing both sides. When that happens transactions come together more successfully.

I knew I wanted to just do ranch sales when I came to PMZ. Mike allowed me the freedom to do that. I didn't have to do floor time or take calls in the office. He didn't saddle me with any of the normal office chores. Mike wants you to go out and be who you are and make things happen.

Before she had two babies, my sister came to PMZ with me. Growing up she knew my heart was in ranches. We thought about names for the business. Realtor® denotes real estate. I wanted to be a unique Realtor®. So Ranch Realtor® just stuck. We trademarked it with the state of California.

It's featured in all of my advertising in the ag publications like the Stanislaus Farm Bureau News, put out by the local farm bureau, of which I am on the board of directors. I'm also in AgAlert, the publication of the California Farm Bureau Federation.

Mike told me I needed to get plugged in with the ag organizations. So I'm on the committee to raise money for high school students to go to college and specialize in ag studies. It stimulates kids to seek a career in agriculture and helps them with the costs of their education.

I just finished serving as president of the ag committee of the Turlock Chamber of Commerce. I'm on two ag panels for the Modesto Chamber. I'm also secretary for the local Turlock Sunrise Rotary Club.

We bought a ranch in Turlock. Mike asked if I would like him to set me up with an office there so I could be closer to my clients and my ranch. Mike said if I went down there I should make sure to plug into the local clubs.

❖

CHRIS SHAW:
PMZ Name Brings Agents Credibility

For more of Chris Shaw's story, take a look at Chapter Three.

I was marginally successful in real estate for approximately 15 years, but I was searching for something that was missing at other brokerage firms. Since coming to PMZ, my income has increased dramatically.

Brand recognition at PMZ adds at least 10 percent to my income. When people who don't know me hear the PMZ name, it gives me greater credibility than if I were from another company. I always feel that during a listing presentation if it comes down to me and someone else and we are evenly matched, the PMZ name guarantees I will be the winning agent. That ties into its advertising presence; PMZ advertises more on radio and in newspapers than any real estate firm.

I've found another advantage in prospecting is advertising on my own in the Modesto Bee and on the Bee's Internet site. When I advertise in these publications, I enjoy the same advertising rate that PMZ receives as a company, which is the lowest the Bee offers because of the company's quantity of advertising. So I enjoy a quantity discount that far exceeds the amount of advertising I do because it is cumulative with PMZ. I also have some billboards around town, especially in areas or neighborhoods where I'm prospecting. They're called "ask-for" ads. They have my name and number. The calls come directly to me.

Advertising accounts for 25 percent of my business. It's crucial for me.

Another advantage of going with a prominent company that advertises extensively is the quality of opportunity or floor time. That's when you work in the office fielding phone calls that result from real estate signs or ads where the caller isn't asking for a particular agent.

Floor time is a waste of time at most companies. At PMZ, you get active leads. You'll periodically receive calls where someone says, "Hi, I want to sell my house. You're with PMZ, can you come list it?" Those are called come list my house calls. They are the easy ones. They come from the strength of the company name, both because of its longevity and reputation and from the advertising and exposure.

I have continued to track the income received from just one floor call I received in 1996, and the various paths it has led me. I've earned more than $75,000 in commissions from that one call. The client likes the job I have done so he keeps coming back when he needs to buy and sell, and he has referred business.

That gentleman didn't know me the first time he called. I was just a voice on the line. The only reason he was willing to work with me was the strength of the PMZ name. The name symbolizes professionalism. So he determined I must be a professional if I was working for this company.

❖

CARLA TORKELSON:
Advertising is 'Hugely Important'

See Chapter Four for more on Carla Torkelson.

Brand recognition—when the community as a whole recognizes the name of the company and its signage—is a huge thing in our business. People list with PMZ because it has market dominance. Mike's signs are phenomenal. The colors and everything about them make a statement.

He also spends a lot on advertising. As an agent, I personally don't have to advertise very much because it's expensive. I don't believe advertising on an agent level really works. But at the broker level it is hugely important. Brokers must have a presence in the market.

Chapter Six

Achieving Financial Security and a Balanced Life

Although real estate brokers are interested in the their agents' performance, few provide agents with wise counsel with respect to creating long-term financial security and achieving a balanced life.

Even though many people in our industry enjoy good incomes, too many of them don't adequately plan for their financial future and end up without economic security when they age. And although many people who come into the real estate business are successful, they end up discovering that the intensity of the career undermines their personal relationships and draws them away from taking proper care of themselves.

Some agents who do well go broke or face serious health problems. That's why planning for financial and personal success is so important. It is why helping agents achieve these goals is an intrinsic part of the PMZ Way. Not only should agents concentrate on being successful in their practices, they need to do it in a way that helps them build wealth and is healthy for themselves and for those around them.

Employees of many modern organizations benefit from a structured environment in which the entity for which they work provides them with the essentials of life, including health coverage and pensions or profit sharing programs. Although income for most of these workers may not be nearly as high as what real estate agents can earn, at least towards the end of the day, when employees are nearing retirement, they can theoretically look forward to some measure of financial security engineered by their employers. That's the advantage of being an employee and working for someone else.

It's different with real estate professionals. Along with all the benefits of being self-employed come real responsibilities. Because agents are the CEOs of their own businesses, they are responsible for creating their own financial security.

You can't start acquiring financial security when you are 65 years old. Buying financial security is a current and ongoing obligation and it must be addressed.

With that in mind, there are some fundamental concerns agents should consistently keep in mind during the years they practice.

• As soon as you receive a commission check, you should immediately put away adequate funds to pay your state and federal income and Social Security taxes on a timely basis. No agent wants to approach the end of the year confronting unpaid tax bills because he or she has spent all of their income.

• As soon as you start in the business, you need to create a tax-deferred retirement account. Most real estate professionals set up a SEP-IRA, or self-employed persons individual retirement account.

Again, agents should fund this account out of every single closing commission they receive. Doing so also provides substantial tax benefits by reducing agents' gross income dollar for dollar by the amount of money they contribute to their plans.

• You should set aside money for savings over and above funds earmarked for the tax-deferred retirement account to accommodate long-term family needs. They can range from purchasing a home and financing your children's college education to investing in real estate or other pursuits.

• The best way to accomplish these goals is establishing a personal or family budget. It should include normal day-to-day living expenses—car payments, rent or mortgage payments—as well as contributions to retirement plans and savings.

• These budgets are essential because they help agents and their families live beneath their means and enable them to invest and save. We live in a very materialistic society. People are inundated on a daily basis with solicitations to consume, spend money and go into debt—especially with the ready availability of credit.

Many professionals in our field get caught up in this material world and spend too much on things they don't really need. Too frequently they end up in vulnerable financial predicaments even though they earn good incomes.

I've known agents making $250,000 a year who have filed for bankruptcy. That can be avoided with a disciplined, intelligent and mature strategy to plan your life.

• Every agent should have a will. When I ask a room full of real estate professionals how many have had wills drawn up, only small percentages raise their hands. Yet having a will is critically important for everyone, particularly for those with small children or substantial net worth. Otherwise, the government will decide what happens to your estate.

• It goes without saying that people in our line of work should own a home. We're in the real estate business. Buying a home is one of the most important investments we can make. And although we certainly may want to refinance from time to time if interest rates drop, it's important to resist the temptation to pull equity out of the house. There is nothing more satisfying than having the residence paid off in full by the time you are 60 or 65 years old. That move can dramatically enhance a family's financial security.

• You should consider purchasing an adequate amount of term life insurance. It is the cheapest form of insurance. You die, it pays. Life insurance should be bought in sufficient volume to cover the needs of those you could leave behind.

I know young agents who are the primary breadwinners in their families and make $150,000 annually. A spouse who works might be earning an additional $30,000 a year. They have three small children, a home mortgage, the usual assortment of bills—and no life insurance. For a very modest price, an agent in this circumstance can buy $2 million worth of term life coverage and know that if anything happens to him or her, the children and the spouse will be well taken care of.

• You also need to take care of yourself physically. There is no question that performing in real estate at a high level involves no small degree of stress. Being physically fit and having good eating habits is critical to maintaining that high level of performance.

Many of the most productive agents are involved in some kind of regular exercise program and are very conscious of their diets.

What's the point of being financially successful if it can't be enjoyed because you end up contracting maladies such as diabetes or heart disease? Many of these health problems can be avoided or minimized with a proper exercise and diet regimen.

• It is also extremely important to strike a balance in your life that involves embracing family and friends. While preparing your weekly plan, purposely set aside time for the significant others in your life. These times should be respected.

This kind of planning is necessary because real estate is not a nine-to-five occupation. If agents don't set aside time to spend with spouses, children and friends, they too often never find the time to do it and end up alienated from those who were closest to them. They may achieve material success, but they end up with no friends or family around with whom to share it. I've seen it happen.

Here are just a few stories from PMZ agents I admire who have made a success out of both their professional and personal lives.

❖

Phil Schmidt: *'Always Pay Yourself First'*

For more of Phil Schmidt's story, take a look at Chapter One.

When I first started in the real estate business I was 23 and had just graduated from college. Mike's dad, Paul Zagaris, hired me. Mike Zagaris wasn't working there yet.

Paul always encouraged people to invest and put money away because there would be pretty lean times given how the real estate market swings. There are peak periods and down periods. During the down times you had better have a nice reserve account in order to sustain yourself, Paul would say.

Putting money away takes a lot, though not all, of the pressure off during slow markets because you have the security of your savings accounts and whatever other investments you have made.

I try to tell new agents what's important, like my daughter, Jill Parks, who has been working with me for two years. During that time she has built up a fairly healthy retirement account by putting away the maximum allowed. My accountant is very proud of her. She is only 25 and she will at some point in her life be buying investment properties.

There's an old saying that goes, always pay yourself first.

Paying yourself first means taking the first 10 percent of each paycheck and putting it away. Then you make ends meet with the balance.

When I first entered into real estate, I thought I would live forever. I didn't invest in a retirement account, although I had purchased some income properties. After about 10 years, my CPA, who is one of my best friends, said I had to be putting money away.

Since then I've put in the maximum, about $40,000 every year. It's substantial now. All the young people in real estate need to face the same reality: the market goes up and down and over the long term you will find yourself ahead of the game if you invest and plan for retirement. Plus the government rewards you through tax benefits for putting money away.

As the end of the year approaches, Mike reminds people that tax season is upon us. "I hope everyone has put money away, at least 10 percent of income, into a retirement account," he says. Mike acknowledges that he can only guide people; it's up to each of us to make the decision. But he highly recommends it and he gives us constant reminders throughout the year.

At the end of each year Mike and our sales manager, Philip Levin, meet individually with each agent to review their goals and objectives for the coming year. They like to see included within everybody's written goals and objectives not only how much money they want to make but what they are going to do with it, including putting money into retirement.

In the middle of the year they review our goals and challenge us: Are we meeting our goals? Are we putting money away? What can they do to assist us?

They always make that offer. These guys care about their agents. Our personal budgets include gas, food, clothing, utilities and mortgage payments. They should also include our investment or retirement accounts, whichever we prefer.

I've been quite disciplined about doing it during the year. In addition, the Zagaris family has been kind in allowing me to invest in some of their properties over time, which has proven very lucrative.

As agents, we're independent contractors, which means we are considered self-employed. Therefore, the government says we will pay quarterly estimated taxes. That means as part of a budget program—in addition to monthly bills and retirement—we need to put one-third of every check away for income taxes, and not touch that money. Again, this doesn't include the 10 percent of income that should be directed into the retirement account.

Setting aside one-third of every paycheck gives us the resources to pay quarterly taxes, including both halves of Social Security.

Another thing an agent has to do is keep a very accurate record of business expenses. A surprising number of people in corporate life don't do that.

In real estate we do have a big overhead. It's important to maintain records because we can deduct legitimate business expenses, but they have to be documented; there has to be a record of them.

What's nice at PMZ is the company keeps very accurate and complete records of all our business expenses, which are substantial—from putting up signs to ordering business cards to postage to long distance business calls to advertising and promotions. The office pays those costs and bills the agent. That makes it very easy come tax time.

It's the agent's responsibility to keep his or her own accurate records on other types of expenses such as cell phones, gas and car payments, and travel and entertainment expenses.

Life insurance is important in our business. As independent contractors, if you're building up a certain amount of wealth should something happen to you the government will want its share. Life insurance protects family members and the estate so they don't have to draw down investments or liquidate assets to pay estate taxes. Plus, if you're the breadwinner in the family and all of a sudden your income is cut off, the family can be faced with serious financial challenges.

People don't think about these things. They think they're immortal or invincible. But it can happen.

A lot of agents don't have disability insurance. If for some reason you can't do your job by selling real estate, all income can end, but the bills will keep coming in. It's important for people to get disability coverage while they're young and they can qualify for it at cheaper rates.

I don't believe in term insurance. I'm one of those people who bought variable life insurance. It is very expensive when you first take it out, but it can never be taken away from you. It never expires. After a certain number of years you don't even have to pay the premiums; you just keep the insurance. It's like having another mutual fund because the money grows. Plus it's tax-free because it is a life insurance policy. You can also borrow on it for low interest rates if you need to.

What I didn't do, and probably should have done, was plan for my daughters' education. I figured I was making and saving enough money to carry through. What happened was when the children were very young, I bought a few homes, thinking I could sell them to raise the money for college. I ended up financing their college costs using cash flow.

Developing a realistic budget and living beneath your means are sound advice. In the world of real estate, with everyone working on commissions, we have to recognize the market's peaks and valleys. Maybe it was because of how I was raised, but it has always been important for me to put as much money as possible away for a rainy day. So I save a lot of money every year.

People will say, "Phil, you don't need to save. You should be investing the money." But savings is my cushion. After being in this business for 30 years and going through different market swings during each decade—remember the '80s when interest rates were 20 percent?—I know I made the right decisions. During these times, I often recalled great advice I received from Paul Zagaris: "Live below your means."

We all know people who spend every dime they make. There's a great book I read called "The Millionaire Next Door," by Thomas J. Stanley and William D. Danko. It shows the contrast between a successful physician who makes a lot of money and the guy next door who has a salary job, but who has budgeted, invested and done all the right things financially. The doctor buys the boat, the second house, the new Mercedes and the country club membership. But when all is said and done, the millionaire is the guy living next door to him.

The message from this book is that overt demonstrations of material wealth are not anywhere as important as planning, budgeting and developing real net worth.

Another lesson I learned early in life was about taking care of myself. I was a swimmer and water polo player in high school and college. There were morning workouts at school every day of the week. Each morning at 6 I'd practice until 8 before going to my first class. Then we'd work out again in the late afternoon. That's just how it was.

You learn how to develop a discipline because managing time becomes so important. Today, every morning I'm up at 4, have a cup of coffee and read the newspaper. I'm at the gym at 5, where I do a lightweight workout and at least 45 minutes or an hour of cardio exercise. Then I'm home, where I eat a healthy breakfast and go off to work. I'm usually at the office by 7:30.

My weight loss and fitness program help me deal with stress during the day. It was always instilled in me to keep in top physical condition if I wanted to be a top performer, regardless of what I was doing and whether the challenges were mental or physical.

Real estate can be stressful. Something needs to help us take the edge off. Eating right and exercising regularly are really important, not just for real estate agents but for everybody. When I occasionally miss working out I don't feel quite as alert as I would otherwise feel.

I also get a great deal of business at the gym. That's not why I go, but you meet a lot of people. It's another way of prospecting. You're around people so long that they'll let me know they want to sell or they know someone who wants to buy and give me the name.

My family has always and will always come first. My daughters were athletes in school and I can honestly say I never missed attending one of their swim meets or water polo games the whole time they went through high school. I'd put them on my calendar along with all the other appointments.

Before our oldest daughter, Jill, who is now my business partner, went to UC Santa Barbara, she played for a few years at Modesto Junior College. As her team traveled around the state, I never missed one of the games.

Our youngest daughter, Jody, was on the national team and traveled to competitions throughout the U.S., Canada and other countries. I couldn't make it to all of her games, but I did go to all the games that were in the United States.

I did all that while still enjoying a very successful career in real estate. With about 99.9 percent certainty, I can say my clients knew when I was going to spend time with my family and they respected that. I never lost business because I had to go to an event where my children were involved. During those years everyone knew that every Tuesday and Thursday, I was at the water polo game. I still go out of town to visit my daughter who lives in Long Beach.

It's not like I was taking two weeks off to vacation in Italy. I was fulfilling my duty as a father, and people understand and appreciated it. My clients certainly understand because I encourage them to spend quality time with their families too. I have clients in international business who travel a great deal out of country. But when they're home, they are devoted family people and I'm proud of them.

When I was younger, before we had children, I was really involved with boards of directors and serving on committees for worthwhile community groups. I feel fortunate in that I paid my dues early because it's important to give back to the community.

I still give back financially through charitable contributions. It's important to do that.

But during the years when my children were growing up, I rarely attended parties or strictly social functions because it was more important for me to be home with my wife and daughters.

Your kids are with you for such a relatively short period of time. We made the most of it. I have no regrets. They're both doing great and I'm so proud.

❖

TIM RHODE: *'Striving for Balance'*

Read more about the story of Tim Rhode in Chapter Two.

For me, taking care of yourself financially and personally is like living within life's wheel—you have to strive for balance. If your career is going well, but you're not putting away for your financial future, your wheel's off track. If you're in a bad marriage or you're having trouble with the kids and things are not as they should be, it's awfully hard to get up in the morning and be the best sales person and human being you can be. Your whole life needs to be in kilter, like the spokes of a wheel.

There are seven areas of balance: career, finances, health and fitness, relationships with family and friends, spiritual life and fun and recreation. You have to pay attention to all areas. I had success in real estate, but my life was out of balance. My health habits were bad.

What's often the case with Realtors® is their careers are going great, they are gung ho, but they let some of the other six areas of balance fall by the wayside. Neglecting them catches up to you. It's not good for long-term success in your business life either.

For me, the key is stepping outside your everyday business reality—listing or selling a house or solving an escrow problem, the day to day stuff—and being able to plan for your future. For me it's all about dreaming. When I'm out getting my physical fitness—usually out in the boonies doing something that is good for my body and mind—I'm thinking about where I want to be one, two, five, 10 years from now. It's something people don't do enough: dreaming, scheming and thinking how I can solve the problems that are in front of me today—and connecting today's dots with where I'm going in the future. I call it big picture dreaming.

There are two sides to achieving financial security: offense and defense.

Offense is the money you make. Defense is living within your means and investing the rest to provide for your future.

Living beneath your means involves, first, knowing what your expenses are. Most people just spend. I know an agent who makes $950,000 a year gross but spends somewhere between $800,000 and $1 million to make the $950,000. She isn't sure just how much.

That's ridiculous. You have to know what it costs you to live.

I'm not talking about living a life of poverty, because most Realtors® make good money. But they spend too much on what it takes to run their business and then they don't take their money and put it in places that will lead to financial security.

The problem I see with most agents on offense

is they go through the real estate yo-yo. They have a couple of good months and then slack off a bit. They go on vacation or spend the money or quit prospecting. Then they react with, "Oh, I've got to go to work again." It's like a roller coaster. Their income isn't steady and they never get ahead.

Mike Zagaris has the solution. He says, "Have a plan and work your plan." It is the most simple, brilliant statement I've ever heard him make. But it's so hard to do because it entails what most people don't want to do, which is prospecting.

Prospecting is difficult. People fear rejection. And it's mundane work. But it is the single most important thing an agent can do if he or she wants to be successful in real estate and achieve financial security.

Defense involves living beneath your means, making extra money to take and aggressively invest in what you know best. It is different for different people.

I would see a property I wanted and thought was a good buy in the late 1980s and early '90s. So I'd write a 60- or 90-day escrow and then go out and make extra money just to buy that property. Now I'm 45 and financially independent, basically done.

Two things are extremely important. First, having a long-term financial plan in writing with monthly and yearly goals, which include what you're going to make.

Second, and this is an absolute must, is knowing your expenses—having a profit and loss statement you can see and study. You're in business. We're self-employed people, but most people don't look at their business like a business.

The plan is the goal. The profit and loss statement is the reality. When you see yourself making extra money, putting it in some form of investment and watching it compound, that is magnificent.

For me, putting money in something I know in my local area meant real estate. I knew that type of investment and it was ancillary to what I do every day.

Another thing I do is read a lot of great books, including "The Richest Man in Babylon" by George S. Clason. It's about a wealthy lender back in ancient Babylon and how he went from slave to the wealthiest lender of his day as well as a teacher. It contains simple principles that are priceless. You can also learn about playing defense from reading the book "The Millionaire Next Door" by Stanley and Danko.

In addition, I get together with my accountant and we play "Cash Flow," a board game like Monopoly, but so much more in depth in offering help on how to achieve financial security. We learn from it. The whole idea of the game is how to get out of the rat race and onto the fast track. The game's creator is Robert Kiosaki, who also wrote the book, "Rich Dad, Poor Dad."

My wife, Tina, and I had been buying mostly single-family homes. When we started playing this game and reading books, we began buying multiple unit rental properties and some commercial property that provide cash flow so at some point our monthly expenses are overtaken by the amount of money coming every month from passive income—income that arrives without having to work for it.

When you arrive at the "fast track," a place in the game, you can go out and do the things you love and dream about even bigger opportunities down the line.

Another issue is personal health. A lot of the top producers in real estate aren't really mentally healthy. They're successful despite themselves because they have so much innate talent. But their success comes from an I'll show you attitude. They are so driven and willing to do whatever it takes to be successful because making money isn't really what drives them; they want to be number one.

I've seen so many people like that. I have been on panels of national experts. They are talented agents but they don't have balance in their lives. Their life's wheel is a little out of kilter.

At one point my wheel was out of kilter too. I was 35 years old, smoking two and a half packs of cigarettes a day, measuring my coffee consumption in pots rather than cups and eating a very unhealthy diet. Ten years ago we started listening to motivational speaker Tony Robbins. I quit smoking and started exercising. I wanted to do more and more things. Last spring, I spent five days in the southern Sierras near the Bishop backcountry, hiking with skis and backpacks. In five days, we climbed five or six 13,000-foot high peaks and skied down them. It was unbelievably physical, lasting from 7:30 a.m. to 7 p.m.

I have run two 26.2-mile marathons. I ran a race 18 miles up Mt. Diablo. I'm an avid snow skier. I love abalone and scuba diving along the North Coast. For abalone, you have to free dive without using air tanks. You go down 15 to 30 feet. I love to mountain bike down pretty wild trails. I'm into any kind of ball sports. I love golf.

I love going out and doing these things. It builds a passion inside me and keeps me physically healthy.

It is extremely important that every part of the wheel is covered. I noticed at one point that by analyzing my wheel friends were low on my personal ratings. So my wife and I intentionally set out to improve this area. We have a group of adult friends we go out with on a biweekly basis. Discovering where your balance is lacking and making a change will go a long way.

Spending time with family goes without saying. I love to have my kids around and spend as much time as possible with them. I'm very proud that in all my years in real estate I never missed a parent-teacher conference or coaching my kids in Little League or boys and girls basketball. My daughter did baton twirling. I either coached my children or went to their events all the time they were growing up. This is a great benefit of being self employed if you make it a priority—which I did.

❖

Victor Barraza:
Building Wealth From Nothing

Learn more about Victor Barraza's remarkable story in Chapter Two.

I've been in real estate for 15 years. Thirty-five years ago, my dad was a bracero farm worker. I was a year and a half into the business when I bought my first rental property. I was still living at home with my parents.

It seemed as if every year I did one or two personal real estate transactions of some type. Whenever an opportunity came up, I'd figure out a way to buy the property for myself, whether it was in addition to the real estate I already owned or I was trading it for one I previously had.

At the beginning, the down payment for these transactions came from the commissions I earned. Later the properties started producing income that I used to buy more properties.

All the homes I purchased have paid for themselves with the rental income they generated. Rents have covered the mortgage payment, including principal and interest, and property taxes. What I had to come up with was money for the down payments.

I started with a little two bedroom, one bath house in west Modesto that I bought for $51,000 back in 1990. Now I own a number of properties, including agricultural farmland and commercial buildings.

I'm amazed by how many agents don't yet own their home. I firmly believe that's one of the first things they need to do so they can, among other benefits, be able to walk the talk. I believe they should own at least a couple of rental properties so they can also walk the talk when they deal with investor clients. Then they'll know what they're talking about out of personal experience, not just theory. If nothing else, the experience would help them to be more successful in their businesses.

For me, when I have extra money in the bank, I tend to become lazy. So I learned a while back not to keep much money in bank accounts. I need to feel a little bit of a pinch to help me stay driven and focused on achieving my business goals. Not keeping much money in checking or savings accounts is an effortless way for me to work harder.

There are so many options for agents when it comes to investing their money. One of the simplest is real estate because we know what happens long term with appreciation. We work in the business so we can easily manage our properties.

The long-term low risk factor for real estate investment is better than other kinds of investment. And it's easier to invest in areas where you have genuine expertise.

All that said, I also believe in diversifying investments and not putting all my eggs in one basket. I try to diversify in real estate. I have residential single-family and multi-family properties as well as agricultural and commercial investments.

My gross holdings were about $51,000 when I started 15 years ago by buying one piece of investment property. Now adding up the gross value of all the real estate would come out to nearly $6.2 million. That doesn't include other types of investments I have.

It is a lot easier for people to get motivated to invest in real estate today than when I started because the market is so good now. When I bought that first house the market was still shaky as to whether it was going up or down. I came in during the late '80s and early '90s when the market was very unstable. I didn't know which way it would head. I decided long term you couldn't go wrong in real estate—even if the market didn't seem to support such a conclusion at that point in time. Also, I decided having excess money in the bank wasn't helping my business grow very much because I was getting too comfortable.

Besides real estate there are certainly other investments people can make. But most of them require paying some other person to handle your money for you. You really have no control over what will be done with the funds. Either your stockbroker or the market will decide what is going to happen. If you want to have some control and be able to increase your holdings, you need to become very educated in order to make wise decisions about where to put your money and when to pull it.

For agents, real estate investment doesn't require four, five or six years of college training in order to have a good sense about how the market is performing and where it is heading. You see that for yourself every day.

As the market changes, there are all kinds of different options for investing and financing real estate. One recent trend is for investors to buy real estate with 100 percent financing.

It was an option that was difficult to find years

ago. It is easy to find nowadays. There have been a lot of investors purchasing investment property with no equity in the homes. It is a wonderful thing if we know the market will continue to climb for a couple of years. In the last three or four years we have seen investors buying with 100 percent financing realizing appreciation of more than $100,000 in equity without having put in hardly any money of their own. It's why so many people have caught onto this method.

But they need to be cautious in going that route because if the market goes down even a little bit, which it inevitably will at some point, these investors could find themselves upside down. We just don't know how much higher the market can go.

Some investors are conservative, others are not. Some want to own less property and have a lot of equity in each one. Others want to own a lot of properties with hardly any equity at the beginning. When you spread your wings out far enough, a little bump on the road can knock you down.

I tell some of my clients who immigrated to the United States with limited English skills and formal education, they can make their money grow just like any university graduate by putting it in real estate. It places a lot of people on an equal footing even if they didn't have the advantage of a good education.

I counsel my clients on their options for investing depending on how much money they have available and their risk level. Those options include real estate, savings and checking accounts, CDs, stocks, mutual funds or opening up their own business. It comes down to what is the safest given their plans. If their plans involve long-term gain, we'll usually discover that real estate is the best option.

I've pointed a number of people into real estate. A lot of my clients who are already real estate investors appreciate the fact we can see eye to eye in finding the right kind of property to invest it. We connect pretty well.

For those who are just getting into the business and want to manage their properties themselves, I supply some of the paperwork they need to get them going: rental agreements and applications, and log sheets to track income and expenses. Or if they don't want to manage themselves, I refer them to property management firms that can handle it for them.

❖

Suzanne Robinson: *Getting High From Helping People*

A highly successful agent, Suzanne Robinson is motivated by something other than money.

My parents and grandparents were all podiatrists, foot doctors, in the Midwest where I was born in Toledo, Ohio in 1942. My grandfather owned a shoe store and movie theater in Ann Harbor, Michigan and co-invented the football cleat with Spaulding. He used the proceeds to go to podiatry school.

I went all the way through school in Toledo and graduated from the University of Toledo with a B.A. in retailing. My husband—now of 38 years—Robert lived nearby. A sister-in-law resided in Danville, California and we loved the weather when we came out on vacation. A job opportunity came up in Modesto for my husband, who is a licensed clinical social worker, which we thought would last for five years.

We loved the Central Valley—the people, the climate; it's two hours from everything. We loved raising our son here. Even though we didn't know anyone at first, we came to love and embrace the community.

When our son was seven I thought about going into teaching. We had lost a child and it was as if I wasn't finished with the nurturing part of life. After serving as a teacher's aide for a year, I realized it wasn't what I needed. I wanted a profession where I could follow my heart. Money is good too; you have to work at something where you get paid.

I went into real estate because I thought I would be helping people fulfill their dreams.

When we first moved to this area, we had a Realtor® who after we came to town said, "Here are three homes in your price range that you can afford. You don't negotiate." There was no give and take at all. She essentially told us, "Here are the three. You pay the price. It's the best you can do."

She never asked what we wanted. It was a very narrow approach to the profession.

Since we were just moving to Modesto, I went along. We did choose a home that was OK. After we moved in we found out the house had belonged to the agent's brother-in-law. The neighbors revealed it had remained on the market unsold for more than a year and a half.

We lived there a year and a half and then got out. Because of the appreciation we didn't lose anything.

I thought to myself: boy, why didn't that Realtor® pay attention? To this day when I see her, I cross my eyes.

I'm a people person. I love helping people. I'm not bashful. I thought through real estate I could have more flexibility with scheduling if I needed it. My husband and son were number one. My profession was number two.

The first few months after I got into the profession, I was absolutely hooked. I loved the constant change. Every day you get to embrace something new. I had the passion. I can truthfully say I love my profession because it is so personally rewarding.

I do like the money, obviously. The profession has been very generous to me. But that is not my main motivation. I get a real high out of helping people solve the puzzle and find their nest. Every home has a feeling. Every home has a special quality.

My dealings with clients come from the heart. All of my clients are referral based because I've been in business for so long. I've sold some people four or five homes. There's the couple that just got married. Then they have their first child and then a second. One couple just sent their children off to college and I'm helping them downsize. You establish real relationships and personal connections with people. They know I've been here for years and I will be here for many more.

I'll talk people into a house as well as talk them out of a property if I feel it's not the right decision. Maybe they shouldn't sell at this time or they'll be too financially stressed if they buy. I express my true feelings because this is a huge investment for most clients and it can be very stressful for some.

If I believe they are getting in way over their heads or the purchase will place too much stress on them or their family, I'll express my opinion.

"Hey, think twice about this," I'll say. "Be cautious."

Oftentimes a client wants to buy a bigger, newer home. I might ask, "Think about it. You'll have to put in new window coverings, a pool or fix up the yard. Those will all be additional expenses. Do you have it in your finances to be able to stretch that far?"

My clientele boast a wide variety of age groups, a variable buffet of clients, because I've been in the business for 25 years.

A number of clients, noting that the city is growing so fast, have expressed a desire to retire and move to the mountains. I'll advise caution or raise questions. I've seen situations where there are longtime residents who have lived and worked here. What they really want to do is travel. They see the prices of homes going up so high and realize they have a nest egg in their property.

After two of my clients moved to the Sierras, their children and grandchildren were too busy to come up and see them very often. Their older friends and relatives didn't drive up a lot either. These former clients found themselves coming down the hill for shopping and medical needs. They ended up moving back. "Why did we sell our house and go away?" they asked.

Every client is special. Each of them has his or her own story. They're like personal friends. I love my clients, regardless of whether they love me.

People ask why I don't retire. I love what I do. I will slow down, but can't see myself retiring unless I can't remember where I am or can't get around anymore.

I do take time off. My husband and I are into balance. We take care of ourselves, travel and visit family. When we do, I know I'm covered at the office. I have a licensed escrow assistant and a wonderful team at PMZ. There are several seasoned agents I know who help each other and know how the other works. It's a wonderful weave.

That's what I love about Mike Zagaris and the Zagaris family. I don't think you can be associated with a harder working real estate family behind the scenes than the Zagarises. They give back to the community and they give back to their agents. They embrace their profession. They love what they do just as I love what I do. That's why I'm here.

When I started off in real estate I was with a major national franchise company because I thought it would open more doors. I could be behind their name. I found out within the first year that this wasn't the case. You're an independent contractor. Clients come to you for your service.

Whenever I used to represent a client and the other agent was with PMZ, I was always pleased because I knew each of its agents was seasoned, got the job done and I didn't have to do their work for them. They performed their part of the transactions and I would do mine. I was impressed.

Twenty years ago I moved to PMZ. I found out later Mike Zagaris had talked to his staff at one of their morning meetings about how his organization was growing. "If there are any agents you've had escrows with who you'd like to come work at PMZ, let me know," Mike asked. "I'll contact them."

Mike called me.

At the time PMZ was a male-dominated office. I loved it because the agents dressed for success. All the guys wore suits and ties. (It's somewhat more casual now.) Everyone had a four-door car—a mobile office—that was cleaned, polished and ready go to.

At first when Mike called and said there was room for me at PMZ, I was concerned. I felt I would have to work harder amid more competition; I wondered whether I could step up to the plate and meet his standards.

Mike is a very quiet, but extremely brilliant guy. He embraces all his agents, understanding what we need in order to do our jobs well. Every week Mike has a morning meeting where he often covers the latest happenings in the world and how they affect our marketplace. He constantly encourages us to think in terms of our own personal growth.

I look forward to the morning meeting every week. I wish they would last longer than a half hour or hour. Mike always listens to what we agents have to say and pays attention. I could listen to him speak for hours. When he addresses groups like the Board of Realtors®, I love to go and hear him.

Shortly after joining the firm, I needed help for one of my clients from PMZ's commercial department. I found a qualified commercial person to help. PMZ is a full-service organization, meaning it's full service for my clients.

They are number one for me. If I have a client whose husband needs to rent commercial space for his business office, I can direct him to many seasoned professionals in our commercial division. If one of my clients wants to buy 100 acres of agricultural land, I have someone who is experienced and can serve him or her at PMZ. If I have clients who are new to town and say they can't yet afford to buy, there is a rental division at PMZ where I can help them get assistance. I can obtain the keys to homes, take them out and show them the rentals.

When I joined PMZ, Mike's father, Paul M. Zagaris, had just passed away. Mike became president of what was renamed PMZ. At that time my husband and I owned a home in a subdivision that was almost paid off. Our accountant said we needed tax write offs. We shouldn't own a house that was paid for, he said.

Paul Zagaris built many of the popular established subdivisions in Modesto. He developed the lots and sold them to builders. He developed Eastridge, Eastridge Plaza, River Heights, Sherwood Forest and Dutch Hollow, where we now live. PMZ was building homes at the time through a custom home division.

We were looking to buy another re-sale home when I talked with Steve Zagaris, Mike's brother, who was building homes for PMZ. He was extremely talented and had a wonderful eye for architecture. Building a custom home from the ground up with Steve's help benefited me a great deal. I saw the flow of construction, the materials, floor plans, how it was built—everything connected with the home. It gave me a deeper appreciation than you get from selling only re-sale homes.

Steve had volumes of information about home building. He would take my husband and I aside and explain anything we wanted to know. He was always up on the latest technologies and was very interested in making new housing more energy efficient. Steve was always a leader in the building industry. He was always taking the next step and looking ahead into the future. He really paid attention to detail.

It was a great loss when we lost him to cancer in 2000. We will always miss him.

It was very comforting to me to find people like Steve Zagaris within the organization. It was reinforcement that I made the right decision to be at this firm.

This love of the profession has carried through to all of us who have worked here over the years. You want to help the people at PMZ and be part of this winning team. They've done very well and been very good to me. And I've been very good to them. It's a two-way street.

Taking time for yourself is also important because you need to have a solid base before you can branch out in the world. Every morning my husband and I have breakfast together. We spend time in the morning chatting about our day. If he has to be at the office at 7 a.m., then we talk at 5:30 or 6 a.m. It doesn't matter. You have to pay attention to these things.

We make time for ourselves. We schedule time off with each other just like we're setting other kinds of appointments. That time can fall on a Tuesday or a Thursday. If one of my clients calls on that day, I say I'm on an appointment; I can't speak with them today but I can be with them on Friday or Saturday.

I do work a lot of weekends because that's when many of my clients can be free. My husband understands. If I have to work on a weekend day, he'll go off to work at one of our duplexes or perform yard work at home.

I'm a big Giants fan and we go to baseball games in San Francisco. Or we take the dogs for a walk and turn off the cell phones. You have to do that.

Having balance in your life also means eating right. I could exercise more, but I take walks and make sure I do yoga. If I'm really stressed, I get on my stationary bike on the gazebo in the back yard so I'm not as anxious.

My husband and I always thought we would live off his income and save mine. It helped too when our son went to UCLA, which wasn't cheap.

We want to make sure our home is paid for, which it almost is. The cars are paid off. We have a variety of investments in our portfolio. Yes, I own some real estate properties and some stocks. Our accountant says we need investments.

Some of our properties are paid for. We don't want to have to depend on Social Security. We desire a nice lifestyle where we can live off our dividends and income. We have always saved a minimum of 10 percent of what we earned. In some years it was as high as 20 percent.

When real estate agents embrace this profession they have to embrace the total picture. Too many agents get into this business because they want to make easy money. They are usually the first ones to leave it. Yes, it does pay well. But you also have to work hard at it. You can't be an order-taker. You have to be a giver—as in giving service.

I stress to those agents just getting into the business that they have to save those paychecks because there are taxes to pay and things to do. I've seen a number of new agents make good money and end up not having the funds to pay taxes at the end of the year.

Still, money is not my motivation. What motivates me is having a passion for what I do. It has also served me well financially. But I would do this job for $5 an hour in a heartbeat.

Our whole office will participate in the lottery. The agents always laugh and say if the office wins the lottery everyone will be in the limousine the next day headed to Sacramento, except Suzanne. I'll be in the office, working.

I think when you're free of financial pressures you have the freedom to help your clients. They know you're dealing with them from the heart and not just because you have a car or house payment to make.

My repeat customers know how I feel. Many times I've had clients interested in buying income property they can have for themselves or their children. If I feel it is a sound investment, I encourage them. "If you don't want to buy it, I will," I'll say. "Or if you don't want it in a year or two, I'll buy it back." And I'm serious.

I want my clients to be comfortable financially, have less stress and prepare for retirement too. I'm not a financial planner, but I am careful to ensure my clients feel good about their real estate investments.

Oftentimes I have relocation clients. I handle clients on behalf of some large companies that are bringing new employees to town. I'll pick up the wife, get in the car and visit all the area schools. Schools are important for families with children. They're coming from different parts of the country.

I don't know the special things they need for their children. I do know which schools have the best test scores. But the families need to visit campuses and get a feel for the pulse of the schools and hear the laughter of the students. I realize they each have their own comfort zone. So I sometimes need to take a little more time with my clients to be sure they get it right.

Chapter Seven

Give Selflessly

It is my belief that what goes around comes around. Agents who give selflessly of themselves to their community are rewarded with their community's embrace. By giving, agents invariably weave themselves into the fabric of their communities and develop both visibility and reputation. By working alongside like-minded people, others gain a positive sense of an agent's character and personality.

We are blessed to be able to live in our country and participate in the exciting and rewarding business of real estate. The least we can do to express our gratitude for these blessings is to give back to the communities in which we live and work.

At PMZ Real Estate we strongly encourage our agents to get involved in community activities. This involvement is an integral part of The PMZ Way.

Agents often ask me what to get involved in. "Start with what you are interested in," I'll respond. If your interest is athletics, consider coaching a little league or soccer team. If your interest is in helping the less fortunate, get involved with one of the many service clubs or charitable organizations in your community. There is a veritable cornucopia of civic, church, political and neighborhood organizations, projects and causes that sorely need volunteers.

We are proud of the work of our PMZ Community Foundation, a non-profit organization that provides substantial financial support to many worthy charities throughout the region. Through foundation events such as the PMZ Joe Rudi Celebrity Golf Classic, our staff makes a difference in the lives of so many.

This past October we raised $50,000 from our golf tournament. I will never forget one agent's contribution in particular. Dennis Nairn won the $2,500 first prize in our raffle. He immediately turned the $2,500 back to the foundation and said to me, "Mike, please give it to a charity that helps children." Dennis exemplifies the selfless giving that reflects the best of our profession.

Through acts of giving and caring that are too numerous to recount here, individual PMZ agents represent the best tradition of giving back to their communities. Here are just a few of their stories.

❖

BEN ALLUSTIARTE:
'Going From Success to Significance'

He makes his contributions through church and service organizations.

My grandparents on my father's side came from Spain, where they were Basque sheepherders. My mom's parents were Portuguese dairy farmers who came from the Azores Islands.

I was born in 1951, in Patterson. When I was in the sixth grade we moved to Modesto, where I graduated from Davis High School.

After three years at Fresno State University, I finished my B.A. degree in economics at California State University, Stanislaus. Then I worked for seven years on my parent's cattle ranch and farm near Fairfield.

In 1981, at age 29, I came back to Modesto and was immediately hired at a mortgage-banking firm where I had worked while in high school.

That was when interest rates were at 18 or 20 percent. There were a lot of foreclosures. Things were getting gloomy.

Phil Schmidt, an agent friend who was with PMZ, encouraged me to get started in real estate. I came there in the early '80s. In the years to come I moved around to a number of different real estate brokers, eventually coming back to work for Mike Zagaris in March 2004.

Meantime, in the mid-1990s, I earned a master's degree in public administration and urban and regional planning from Cal State Stanislaus and got a CCIM, becoming a Certified Commercial Investment Member, from the National Association of Realtors®. There are only 7,500 CCIMs in the country; it's similar to completing a master's program specializing in commercial real estate.

I'm with PMZ because I know it's number one in the region. It also gives me more latitude. At other broker offices you have to either do residential or commercial real estate. There is no in-between. With PMZ, because it has a commercial division, Mike lets me do both.

Getting involved in the community allows real estate agents to move to the next level. Any agent can achieve a level of business success and be happy or not so happy. But you go from success to significance when you do a lot of community service. In that way you take your level of success and your self worth to the next level. It gives you purpose. That change of focus offers an internal motivation that comes from each man or woman's need for personal growth.

For the last 10 years I have been active with the Kiwanis Club of Modesto. We raise money for the Salvation Army and do building and remodeling work for Laura's House, a halfway house in Modesto helping women with drug and alcohol problems get off the streets so they can get their children back. Laura's House is a facility with four or five older houses sharing a common backyard. It includes a doublewide modular set up with computers so women can earn their GED certificates. It also hosts Alcoholics Anonymous and Narcotics Anonymous meetings.

Kiwanis was awarded the grant money to put up the facility, including the modular. We also go out there and help with the physical maintenance work and provide funds.

Our Kiwanis Club puts on pancake breakfast and wine and cheese events with the proceeds directed to worthy local causes. We've helped build a Boy Scouts clubhouse, helped supply life jackets for the Sheriff's Department and sent money to the Sea Scouts in Stockton.

In addition, I'm on the board of directors for the Modesto Junior College Foundation. It conducts annual fundraising to raise money for scholarships to aid students and further the goals of the college itself and its two campuses.

I'm involved with Our Lady of Fatima Catholic Church Men's Club in central Modesto. The church has its own school and we do fundraising for the church and the school. Our major focus in the last couple of years has been building a new gymnasium. It is a $2 million project and I've worked with a lot of nice people on that committee.

Then there's the Knights of Columbus, another men's group connected with the church. I also participate in annual events to raise money for Central Catholic High School in Modesto. Funds benefit everything from athletic programs to classrooms and computers for the school.

Being active is a matter of connecting with people in different organizations. You do it from the heart. It's about enriching your life.

However, in the process you're also networking and meeting with many people who believe as you do. The first two years I was at Kiwanis I didn't meet anybody who brought me business. Then it just took off. Today I probably average between 10 and 20 transactions a year from fellow Kiwanis members or people who know me through the club.

For me involvement with the church groups is a spiritual thing. But I also get clients from church activities.

Once you acquire a clientele from a church or other type of organization, you want to give back more than you would have if you weren't getting any business. It creates a challenge within yourself to strive for a more unique sense of meaning in your life—a challenge to grow personally.

I always give 110 percent of myself to my clients. But you make sure you go the extra mile for people you meet in these organizations once they become business clients because, you see, they also become friends for the long term.

I do a lot of mail-outs and advertising too, going after non-owner occupied or investment properties. Yet most of my business today is referral based.

❖

JEANNIE MACDONALD: *Real Estate is About People, Not Money*

From a prominent Modesto family, Jeannie MacDonald learned at an early age about the duty to give back.

I was born Modesto in 1945. My father was in the grocery business. At one time he had three stores in Modesto called Angelo's Markets. My mother was a homemaker. After finishing Downey High School I attended Stephens College in Columbia, Missouri, where I got a degree in sales and marketing.

I went to work for women's clothing stores in California, starting in Modesto and then in Southern California, where I met my husband, Tom MacDonald. His work took him to St. Louis, Missouri, where I worked for clothing stores in the Midwest and eastern seaboard.

After our first child was born, we moved back to Modesto in 1973. Mike Zagaris' father, Paul Zagaris, and my father were very good friends. Paul had offered my husband, Tom, a job. So Tom took the class in real estate, passed the test and went to work for Paul Zagaris selling real estate. I worked in our family's grocery business, mostly purchasing gourmet food and cookware products.

The grocery stores were sold when my father passed away. I came to work with Tom. At the time there was no such thing as assistants and transaction coordinators for real estate agents. I was probably one of the first personal assistants. I handled Tom's marketing and transactions starting in 1988.

By 1990, I had my own license. So in addition to my other duties, I also started selling. Business was great. I've always been very active in the community so it was very easy to market us because people were very familiar with my family's name, Angelo, and the MacDonald name.

The Angelo family philosophy that was passed on to me is that we give back to the community that supports us.

I'm on the board of trustees for Memorial Hospital. I've been involved with Omega Nu, a women's sorority in town that does a lot of fundraising for community projects. I have been on the board of directors for the Center for Human Services, working mostly with children in crisis and providing family counseling. I'm also on the board for the Family Service Agency, a similar type of organization.

Plus I'm very involved in a Realtor®-sponsored community event called Christmas CanTree, which raises money and collects donated food items for the Salvation Army. This event started here in Modesto through the Realtor® community and has spread nationwide.

We do a lot of fundraising in real estate. We raise money for Community Housing and Shelter Services, which gets donations of housing and clothing for the homeless in the community. I've been on the boards of a number of similar groups over the years.

It's part of a family tradition that was instilled in me. There is tremendous self-satisfaction from doing it. It makes me feel good.

Name recognition is very important in real estate. If you're out in the community doing worthwhile things, people come to know you. And they want to do business with people like them. So when it comes time to buy or sell a house, they think, Jeannie and Tom MacDonald are just like us. Why not do business with them?

When you've been active in the community and

in business for 30 years, like my husband has, there are a lot of referrals. It's not the reason you get involved in the community, but it's certainly one outcome.

I like to let other people take the glory for the work we do. It's not my thing. I enjoy the job we're doing together. I love what I do.

Real estate also should never be about the money. It should be about the people. It can be about the money, but then you don't get the genuine sense of satisfaction that comes from helping others in need.

What's really fun when you've been in the business these many years is when we sell to second-generation clients. Now the children of previous clients are turning to us when they want to buy and sell real estate.

That's great. It's what you work for. It is the kind of business you want to create over the long term: having people so satisfied with what you do that they repeatedly refer to you and use you for their own personal needs.

❖

KRISTI ENGEL: *'By Giving to Others, It Gets Back to You'*

For more on Kristi Engel's story see Chapter Three.

I tried to keep my personal and business lives separate when I first started in real estate. As I got into it more I discovered that is difficult to do in our profession.

At first you feel guilty: Why should I do business with friends? I don't want them to think I'm involved in church or school activities just to generate business for myself.

But I found when I'm providing these people with good real estate services, they trust me, feel safe, taken care of and well represented. So it's a win-win situation.

I am someone who is involved in activities because of my children. I discovered during my first year in real estate more than 30 percent of my business came from my sphere of influence: friends, family and acquaintances. They do overlap with your business affairs. That is also the part of my business that has grown.

For example, I recently listed a home after meeting the people because our four-year old daughter does gymnastics with their daughter. I wasn't out there at gymnastics events soliciting their business. But they have to relocate out of state and need to sell their home. They later told me they weren't sure whom to call but trusted me. It comes back to trust. From meeting and knowing me, they concluded I was competent.

You should not get involved in the community because you think it will grow your business. Then you're doing it for the wrong reason.

I'm incredibly involved in my church and children's school and in sports with friends and neighbors who like to be outside. At least 40 percent of my business this year has come from people I've met through those activities. It wasn't because I deliberately marketed myself that way. It just came.

I am a member of the Church of the Cross, an interdenominational church in Modesto. One of its primary activities this year is the outreach committee. Because of my relationship to real estate I have access to area maps and addresses. It's helpful for the outreach committee that focuses on neighborhood activities. We're known for a huge Easter celebration we put on in the neighborhood around the church as well as a Christmas program.

Through the church, I have met many people who have relocated here and have had me help them find homes to live in as a real estate agent. I don't actively advertise to them that I'm an agent. That's not why I'm active. I'm at church because I want to be and because I believe in God. But conversations do ensue and people find out I'm in real estate.

I make contributions to my church. By giving to others it gets back to you tenfold.

It's been the same thing with my son's school. Keaton is in junior high school. I assist in the classroom as a parent helper. I help in the library. I help with several of the fundraising events. The biggest is an annual golf tournament. Last year we raised $100,000. Through all the sports events I'm either the car pool mom or I'm donating food or drinks, whatever is needed.

As a parent it's hard for me to imagine not being involved. I don't do it because I think someone will want me to handle a real estate transaction. But that comes along too. One parent from school bought a ranch through me. Several have listed investment properties through me. I met them and came to know them through school. You get around to talking about what everyone does. They find out.

I'm also involved with a very informal ladies group that meets somewhere for lunch every other week. I met this network of women through school and a variety of other avenues. We are big believers in women promoting women.

Some are stay-at-home moms. Others run at-home businesses: Mary Kay cosmetics, spa products, clothing lines and mortgage lending. One gal is a CPA. The common thread is supporting each other in our careers and at home. We gather to promote, support and encourage whatever we're doing at work or at the house.

One week five ladies will show up for lunch. Two weeks later there may be 15. It's very informal. We call ourselves a circle of friends.

I've had a significant amount of referral business come through that ladies group.

My life is an example of how giving to others, either individually or through organizations, comes back to you. I'm a very strong Christian and that is an important part of Christian philosophy.

❖

Eric Ingwerson: *'Making a Big Difference'*

Eric served for years as a public official in his native Ceres, where he still lives.

I was actually born here in Ceres in 1954, and never left. My father was a meat cutter for a while and then part owner and manager of a liquor store in Modesto. My mom was a housewife for many years and also worked at the local drug store.

I graduated from Ceres High School in 1972. I was going to go to Modesto Junior College, but was really tired of school. So I was hired at Delta Brands, the Budweiser distributor in Modesto. Back then Budweiser wasn't as popular as it is today so I would be laid off in the winter months when beer sales were slow.

Then I worked for McMahan's furniture store as an assistant on the delivery truck. I was promoted to assistant warehouseman, then head driver on the delivery truck and then head warehouseman. At age 20, I started in furniture sales, working in the warehouse Monday through Friday, and working Saturdays in sales while I learned to sell. I became assistant manager for the McMahan's store in Modesto and later went to work as a salesman for Rice furniture store, also in Modesto.

My uncle, Don Sanders, was a real estate broker. He said there wasn't much of a future in the furniture business. He kept talking to me about getting into real estate. By then I was 25 and married to my high school sweetheart, Carol.

One day a friend, Randy Huggins, a real estate agent who was a couple of years younger than I, came by the furniture store driving a brand new Cadillac El Dorado. It looked like a big boat. "Eric, I just paid cash for this car," he told me. "You've got to get into real estate."

So in 1980, my wife and I borrowed $20,000 by taking out a second mortgage on our house with a 13 percent interest rate and 15 loan points. I didn't have a clue what a loan point was then. The payments were interest-only with a balloon payment due after three years. I was handed a check for $16,800, representing the $20,000 loan less the loan points.

We lived on that money. I quit my job at the furniture store and went to school full time to take the real estate exam, attending classes every day at the former Anthony Real Estate School in Modesto. I took the test and passed it.

I went to work in 1981 for the uncle of Randy Huggins, my friend with the new car. The real estate market had just come off a boom during the late 1970s. I got into it when it hit the skids. The prime interest rate soared to 22 percent that year.

It was very difficult to survive the first two or three years. My wife worked full time as a dental assistant while I sold real estate and worked seven days a week nonstop doing what I could to make a deal. I made $13,000 the first year in business. We were excited with the thought I was making any money at all during that time.

No one wanted to do new financing because the interest rates were so high. We took motorcycles and boats as down payments. Every deal had to be put together with loan assumptions. You could legally assume loans in those days. We would carry a loan to serve as our commission, collecting the money in monthly payments because there wasn't enough cash generated in the transaction to pay the agent. I would sell my notes for 50 cents on the dollar to my own broker in order to raise enough money to pay the monthly bills.

Things became better. Interest rates dropped to 12 percent in 1984, and everyone celebrated. When interest rates came down it made it easier to get loans to buy homes. (Later on they passed a law banning the assumption of loans without qualifying for them.)

I made $40,000 in 1985. I thought to myself, This is living. I went down and bought a new 1986 Chrysler Fifth Avenue, the first time in my life I owned a new car.

The agency I worked with closed down and I went to work for another broker under a national franchise name in 1988. I had no interest in leaving Ceres for a larger office. I worked two blocks from where we lived. Things were going well.

One day in 1994, I got a call at home from Mike Zagaris. I wasn't interested in switching over to PMZ. He persisted. "Give me 20 minutes," Mike said. "If you don't like what I have to say I'll never bother you again."

I drove to Modesto, met with him and after 20 minutes he convinced me to quit where I was at in Ceres and go to work for the Zagarises.

That was the best move I ever made in my real estate career. I've been more successful in my time at PMZ than I ever was at any of the other offices where I worked. I didn't realize what I was missing: the great support staff, the advanced technology, the continuing training for agents and the opportunity for business expansion.

In 1997, PMZ opened an office in Ceres. I was the sales manager for six agents. Now we have 28.

My own business has definitely increased. Before coming to PMZ, in my best year I made $60,000. Every year at PMZ it went up. I earned $100,000 my second year at PMZ. Now I am at more than twice that amount. Overall, it's gone up four-fold.

Much of the credit also goes to community participation.

In 1982, the father of a longtime friend, Jim Cooper, asked me to attend a meeting of the Ceres Lions Club. I didn't know if I wanted to be part of the Lions Club. I considered it a bunch of older guys and didn't think I'd fit in. After first turning down the invitation, I went to a meeting.

Surprisingly, there were younger guys there too. I wasn't at all thinking of joining a service club to enhance my business. At that point I joined the Lions Club thinking I'd stay with it to do my civic duty or help the community for a year or two and then get out.

That was in 1983. By 1989, I was president of the club and I'm still a member.

The Lions Club is a service organization that raises funds for community projects, from Boy Scouts and youth sports to completing improvements at local parks to helping other groups.

During that time, two people—the mayor and my neighbor, Greg Smith, who is also in real estate—asked me to serve on the city of Ceres Planning Commission. Greg said being on the commission would keep me in touch with what is going on and allow me to know where all the new development was going in.

I applied and was appointed by the City Council in 1988. So often people live in the same small town all their life and never have a clue about what's happening around them. By becoming a planning commissioner, I could see where development was going and who was building what and where. Of course, if a matter before the commission had anything to do with the real estate company where I was working, I immediately excused myself to avoid even the appearance of a conflict of interest. That happened only occasionally. Where it helped me to serve was gaining first-hand knowledge of what was happening because I was voting on it.

After seven years on the Planning Commission, I ran and was elected to a seat on the City Council in 1995. I served until 2003. I also served nearly two terms as mayor of Ceres. In addition to elected office, I also served as a member of the board of directors of the Ceres Chamber of Commerce.

Public service was a challenging experience. Being on the council, more so than the Planning Commission, not only kept me on the cutting edge of growth, but also allowed me to become a policy maker helping to shape the city and community into a better place.

I think I helped make a big difference. During my tenure on the council we grew economically and industrially, expanded the Fire Department, brought in a huge new grocery distributor, created jobs and purchased property where a new community center will be built. We expanded the park system and youth recreation. We renovated the city's rundown baseball complex.

There are negative talkers who like to complain that the City Council has real estate people on it who are in it just to bring in more housing and developers. I was convinced that we needed to grow in Ceres in a positive way. That involved expanding our economic base as well as our housing stock.

All this involvement helped me because everyone knew I was a real estate agent. It opened doors. They'd say, "Eric sells real estate. Let's give him a call." I was introduced to so many people I would never have met otherwise. It created a client base that turned into a big part of my business.

Agents who are new to an area will engage in prospecting. They will often open the phone book and start calling people in the community. It's tough duty. You get a lot of rejection.

I didn't realize it while it was happening, but I was doing my prospecting in Ceres through my meetings and acquaintances made at the Lions Club, the Chamber of Commerce and the City Council.

Now I teach a class for new agents at PMZ University. I ask the students, "How are you going to get your name out to people who don't know you?" Then I ask, "How many of you belong to a service club or a local chamber of commerce?" Not many hands go up.

I then advise, "Join one. Call the chamber. They are always looking for new volunteers. Become involved in your community. Pretty soon people will come to know who you are and what it is you do for a living because you're going to get chances to tell them at various functions and events."

I also tell the new agents that by doing these things, the community will get to know and trust them through activities that don't involve real estate. It certainly helps if clients already know and trust you when they need to be represented in the biggest investment they'll make in their lives: the buying or selling of their home.

❖

Joseph Bondi: *'Opening the Door'*

See more of Joseph Bondi's story in Chapter Three.

Everybody knows I'm Catholic. It works well for me. You see subtle Catholic things in my office: An eight-inch high statute of Our Lady. A small cross is above the door. They don't overpower.

I help out through the local diocese with a Catholic retreat, Journey in Christianity, to bring people closer to God. I also work with a small nonprofit group called Civitan that provides services to other groups, like supporting the Walk for Life and the Howard Training Center in Modesto.

It's all been very rewarding for me. I never ask for business from the people I meet when I'm doing this work, but they bring it to me. Once they open the door to conversation, I tell them what I do and it produces business.

About The Author

Michael P. Zagaris was born and raised in California's Central Valley. He received his B.A. degree in economics with honors from the University of California, Santa Cruz and his Masters in Business Administration from Santa Clara University.

Prior to joining his family's real estate business in 1977, Zagaris worked in management positions at Xidex Corporation in Sunnyvale, California and Memphis, Tennessee as well as ALZA Corporation in Palo Alto.

He presently serves as president and CEO of PMZ Real Estate. In addition, he is president of Zagaris Management Services, a family-owned land development firm, and president of Qualified Mortgage Services, a family-owned mortgage company. Zagaris is also chairman of Pleasanton, California-based Assay Technology, a leading developer of disposable analytical tests used to monitor indoor air quality. He is chairman of Directline Technologies in Modesto, a leading nationwide provider of telemarketing services for colleges, universities and nonprofit organizations. He is co-founder and co-owner of CentralValleyJobs.com, the leading on-line job site in the Central Valley.

In addition, Zagaris serves as chairman of the PMZ Community Foundation, a nonprofit charitable organization. He is founder and president of Modesto Art in Public Places, a nonprofit organization dedicated to providing permanent art installations within parks and other public properties in that city. He is a member of the board of directors of Doctors Medical Center in Modesto and chairman of the Ancient Hellenic Arts Council of the Fine Arts Museums of San Francisco.

Mike Zagaris lives with his wife, Midge, in Modesto. Their five children are grown and they are now enjoying their grandchildren.

He can be contacted at 209-548-4510 or at mzagaris@pmz.com.

About
PMZ Real Estate

PMZ Real Estate is the largest provider of real estate services in Central California. Paul M. Zagaris, who began his real estate career in 1947 in Modesto, founded the company. This family-run independent real estate firm is now owned by Paula Zagaris Leffler, Jon Zagaris and Michael Zagaris.

With annual sales of well over $1 billion, PMZ Real Estate is among the top 100 real estate companies in the United States. It provides residential brokerage, commercial/industrial brokerage and property management services.

Additional information about PMZ Real Estate is available at www.pmz.com.